WRITERS AND CRITICS

Chief Editors
A. NORMAN JEFFARES
R. L. C. LORIMER

Advisory Editors
DAVID DAICHES   C. P. SNOW

ALBEE

C. W. E. BIGSBY

OLIVER AND BOYD
EDINBURGH

OLIVER & BOYD LTD
Tweeddale Court
Edinburgh 1

First published 1969

Paperback 05 001776 4
Hardback 05 001777 2

Printed in Great Britain
for Oliver and Boyd Ltd
by Robert Cunningham and Sons Ltd
Alva
Scotland

CONTENTS

ACKNOWLEDGMENTS

Acknowledgments are due to all those who have helped and encouraged me in this project. In particular I am indebted to Brian Lee, Jonathan Raban, David Gallon, Raymond Stephens, Tom Warren and Allen and Rhieta Prowle, who have frequently offered helpful advice and constructive criticism.

I am also heavily indebted to the Headmaster and staff of Choate School for their generosity in providing photocopies of Albee's early work and for their ready response to all my enquiries.

Finally my thanks must go, as always, to my wife Pam.

Portions of this book have appeared in *Modern Drama* and *Twentieth Century Literature*. I gratefully acknowledge permission to use them here where they appear in revised form.

The photograph on the front cover is reproduced by permission of Cameta Press.

TO MY PARENTS

FIRST PERFORMANCES
OF ALBEE'S PLAYS

The Zoo Story: Schiller Theater Werkstatt, Berlin, 28 Sep. 1959.

The Death of Bessie Smith: Schlosspark Theater, Berlin, 21 Apr. 1960.

The Sandbox: The Jazz Gallery, New York, 15 Apr. 1960.

The American Dream: York Playhouse, New York City, 24 Jan. 1961.

Fam & Yam: The White Barn, Westport, Conn., 27 Aug. 1960.

Who's Afraid of Virginia Woolf?: Billy Rose Theatre, New York City, 13 Oct. 1962.

The Ballad of the Sad Café: Martin Beck Theatre, New York City, 20 Oct. 1963.

Tiny Alice: Billy Rose Theatre, New York City, 29 Dec. 1964.

Malcolm: Schubert Theatre, New York City, 11 Jan. 1966.

A Delicate Balance: Martin Beck Theatre, New York City, 22 Sep. 1966.

Everything in the Garden: Plymouth Theatre, New York City, 16 Nov. 1967.

Box-Mao-Box: Buffalo Studio Arena Theatre, Buffalo, 7 Mar. 1968.

CHAPTER I

LIFE AND EARLY PLAYS

Edward Franklin Albee III was born in Washington, D.C., on 12 March 1928. At the age of two weeks he was adopted by Reed and Frances Albee and taken to live in a Tudor stucco house in Westchester, New York. Reed Albee was the millionaire owner of a chain of theatres started by his father, Edward Franklin Albee II. At one time the family had control of some seventy vaudeville theatres, with an interest in a further three hundred; and, although the business was eventually sold to R.K.O., the family's connexion with the theatre meant that their Westchester house was often full of theatrical personalities.

For the most part Albee lived the life of a spoilt rich boy, with servants, private tutors, and winter visits to Florida and, less exotically, Arizona. With a St Bernard dog to pull his sleigh in winter and a Rolls Royce to take him around town, the young Albee tended equally to precocity and corpulence. At the same time his family life left something to be desired. His father, who died in 1961, tended to be taciturn and to defer to his wife, who, twenty-three years younger and almost a foot taller than her husband, is remembered as striding around in riding clothes and a hard hat, carrying a riding crop. (It is not too difficult to see in his foster-parents elements of the characters he was later to create in *The American Dream*.) The one member of the family with whom he really felt at home was Mrs Albee's mother, Grandma Cotta. Albee, who dedicated his short play *The Sandbox* to her, on her death in 1960, and who draws a portrait of

her both in that play and in *The American Dream*, has
said: "I could communicate with her . . . she was at the
end of it and I was at the beginning so both of us were
outside the ring."[1] For all the difficulties of his childhood,
he has frequently insisted that he feels no resentment
towards his adoptive parents; but the "deep-seated
resentment"[2] which he still feels against his natural
parents is all too apparent in the contempt with which he
treats the family unit in virtually all of his plays.

Educationally Albee's record was extremely poor. In
five years he was dismissed from two schools and one
college. After attending Rye County Day School until
the age of eleven, he was sent, in September 1940, to
Lawrenceville, a boarding school in New Jersey. Although
he was active in drama and the junior newspaper, he
resolutely ignored his academic work and eventually
failed in four out of five courses. The school recognised
that many of his difficulties sprang directly from his
home situation, but as a result of his academic failure had
to dismiss him in February 1943. His mother viewed this
failure simply as a result of poor discipline and attempted
to correct the fault by submitting him to the rigours of the
Valley Forge Military Academy. To Albee, though, the
school rapidly became known as the Valley Forge
Concentration Camp, while its patriotic boast that
"from the training fields of Valley Forge go men who
will preserve America" left him unimpressed. Indeed,
evidently finding the preservation of America beyond his
immediate capacity, he was once more invited to leave;
and in the autumn of 1944 he entered Choate School,
whose alumni include John F. Kennedy, Adlai Stevenson,
Chester Bowles, and John Dos Passos. Here, for the
first time, he settled down content that he was in a school
in which "they didn't believe in overdiscipline, they just
let you come to your own conclusion that you were

[1] Anon, "Albee: Odd Man in on Broadway", *Newsweek*, 4 Feb.
1963, p. 51.   [2] *Ibid.*

making a fool of yourself".[3] Here, too, he began to take his own writing seriously and found masters who were prepared to encourage him. At Valley Forge, when he had tried to read a poem to a teacher, he had had to break off while the master thrashed another boy across the hands with a riding-crop. Now, however, he wrote sometimes up to eighteen hours a day and produced a large number of poems, short stories, and even a play and a 538-page novel, the latter called *The Flesh of Unbelievers*. At the end of his first year one of his poems, "Eighteen", was accepted by *Kaleidograph*, a Texas literary magazine. His English teacher at Choate has said: "I remember sitting hour after hour in my study with him reading his many, big hand-filled pages. One night I was faced with fifty of them."[4]

The poetry which Albee produced in these large quantities at Choate is largely rather banal and uninspiring. While clearly influenced by the nineteenth-century romantic poets, he failed to adapt their vision or language to his own purpose, tending rather to lapse into a purely adolescent bombast, "Oh, Shakespeare, let me walk abroad with thee."[5]

But while for the most part dull and unrewarding, his poems do throw an interesting light on the young Albee's ideas. Thus the dramatist who was later to insist on the need for man to face the real world as it is, expresses an essentially romantic attachment to illusion in a sonnet called, "To a Maniac". This accepts madness as an entirely legitimate strategy for avoiding the brutality and apparent bleakness of the real world—a point which he was flatly to refute in *A Delicate Balance*.

For you
The earth, its purpose inconceivable,

[3] Geri Trotta, "On Stage: Edward Albee", *Horizon*, IV (1961), p. 79.   [4] "Albee: Odd Man in on Broadway", p. 51.
[5] Edward Albee, "Sonnet", *The Choate Literary Magazine*, XXXI (1945), p. 60.

> Is cast aside, and in its place, a new,
> A happy world, a planet understood
> By you alone, becomes a fact. Who could
> Dispute your right to dream?[6]

This early work, however, does contain evidence of that
optimism which emerges as an essential aspect of his
later work. For, while fascinated by the figure of the
disillusioned man seen at the centre of a decaying world,
he refuses to acknowledge the right to complete pessimism. In yet another sonnet, "Nihilist", he attacks the
solipsistic nature of nihilism.

> Upon his pedestal of self he strikes
> The pose of studied carelessness, or plays
> The role with Judas-like humility,
> Of priest confession to his following
> With Santayanian finesse he spikes
> Existing principles, old, trusted ways,
> And offers in their place sterility
> Of soul and thought; these are his plundering.
> What causes him to mouth the purple grape
> Of life experience, then spit the seeds
> Back at the world? His shouting at the skys,
> His quarreling with God will not escape
> The judgements of his work. His shout recedes,
> His pedestal collapses and he dies.[7]

Scott Fitzgerald has said:

The talent that matures early is usually the poetic
[type] . . . The prose talent depends on other factors
—assimilation of material and careful selection of it,
or more bluntly: having something to say and an
interesting, highly developed way of saying it.[8]

[6] Edward Albee, "To a Maniac", *The Choate Literary Magazine*,
XXXII (1946), p. 71.

[7] Edward Albee, "Nihilist", *The Choate Literary Magazine*, XXXII
(1946), p. 22.

[8] Andrew Turnbull, *The Letters of F. Scott Fitzgerald* (London 1964),
p. 85.

Certainly Albee's first literary efforts were largely confined to poetry, and he continued to think of himself primarily as a poet until well into his twenties. Not unnaturally the short stories which he wrote at this time demonstrated just that remoteness from real life which Fitzgerald had implied was the mark of an immature writer. They demonstrated, too, an uncertain control of language, a prolixity which is reminiscent of his poorer poems. His story "Well, It's Like This", for example, begins with the rather breathtaking sentence: "Adam squinted slightly as the dull, relentless, throbbing sun rays speared downwards, spun and twisted grotesquely on the long thin barrel. . . ."[9] Only in passages of dialogue do we really find the beginnings of that measured articulateness which characterises his later drama.

According to Albee, his dramatic career started at the age of twelve, when he wrote a three-act farce, "the action of which occurred aboard an ocean liner, the characters of which were, for the most part, English gentry and the title of which was, for some reason that escapes me now, *Aliqueen*".[10] The first play which is actually available to us today is the one-act play which he wrote at the age of eighteen and which was published in the *Choate Literary Magazine* for May 1946. A strictly naturalistic drama, *Schism* is concerned with the successful attempt of a young man, Michael Joyce, himself disillusioned with the Catholic Church, to wean a young Irish-Catholic girl away from her family. Alice Monohan, the young girl, confuses her love for him with an acceptance of his ideas and echoes his cynicism without herself really sharing or understanding it. When he suggests that they should run away together she eagerly consents, although in doing so she deserts her dying grandmother.

[9] Edward Albee, "Well, It's Like This", *The Choate Literary Magazine*, xxxii (1945), p. 31.
[10] Edward Albee, "Preface", *The American Dream and The Zoo Story* (New York 1963), p. 7.

At the end of the play, in an excessively melodramatic incident, the young man finally confronts this old woman, who, in a desperate attempt to stop her grand-daughter leaving, has struggled out of her wheelchair. She collapses, and, rather than risk a change of heart on Alice's part, he conceals the dying woman in an adjoining room. As she lies dying, the young couple leave, consoling one another with the thought that "We're not wrong . . . we're just searching for happiness",[11] an implied criticism of a society which urges people to pursue happiness at the expense of common humanity.

While *Schism* clearly demonstrates an understanding of the essence of dramatic conflict, the dialogue is uncertain, and the action constantly verges on melodrama. It is not enough, for example, that the young man attacks Alice's principles. He has to take her crucifix away from her as well, explaining his action in a speech which gives evidence, not merely of his own pretentiousness, but also of Albee's as yet imperfect control of idiom: "It's like a heavy chain around your neck, weighing you down so you can't stand up straight and really see God. I want to help you stand up straight."[12] At the same time Albee shows here a marked tendency to rely on the stereotype, even admitting as much in his description of the charac-ters. One is an "almost typical representative of the lower-middle-class", while another is a "representative of the Irish washer-woman, fat, jovial and somewhat sloppy"[13]—a description not likely to endear him either to the literary critic or the Irish.

Nevertheless he is clearly conscious of more funda-mental ambiguities. The real subject of his play is the lack of compassion which underlies both the authoritari-anism of the Catholic Church and the young man's revolt. Hence the schism which he is demonstrating is not that within the Monohan family or that within a church

[11] Edward Albee, "Schism", *The Choate Literary Magazine*, XXXII (1946), p. 110.　　[12] *Op. cit.*, p. 95.　　[13] *Op. cit.*, p. 87.

threatened by the cynicism of a new generation. The real dissonance is between the human need for understanding and hope, and a system which demands either spiritual submission or moral irresponsibility. His target, therefore, is both the Catholic Church, which "restricts free thinking or unregulated action",[14] and the American Dream, which justifies inhumanity in the name of "a golden future".[15]

On leaving Choate in 1946, Albee moved to Trinity College, a small institution in Hartford, Connecticut. Here he tried his hand at acting, taking the part of the Emperor Franz Joseph in Maxwell Anderson's *The Masque of Kings*, but as a result of his failure to attend either maths lectures or chapel, "the college suggested that I not come back, which was fine with me".[16] With the exception of a brief enrolment at Columbia University for six months in 1949, and another equally brief spell at Washington University, this brought his formal education to an end.

At the age of nineteen, while still living with his parents in Larchmont, Albee now secured his first job, writing continuity material for the music programmes on radio WNYC. After a year at home, during which he became engaged and then rapidly disengaged, he found that life was getting intolerable; and after a particularly virulent and petty row with his parents he left to live on his own, settling in an apartment in lower Manhattan.

The ten years between his twentieth and thirtieth birthdays have been called his bohemian decade, although Albee himself prefers to call them his "pudding years". During this time, in spite of an inheritance of $250 a month, he took a series of temporary jobs, working as an office-boy for an advertising agency and as a salesman in the record department at Bloomingdales. He also worked in Gimbels' book department, as a

[14] *Op. cit.*, p. 95.   [15] *Op. cit.*, p. 110.
[16] Anon, "Albee", *The New Yorker*, 25 Mar. 1961, p. 31.

barman in the Manhattan Towers Hotel, and, for three years, as a Western Union Messenger.

Meanwhile he continued to write, producing both drama and poetry. His connexion with William Flanagan, a young composer with whom he shared his apartment and who later wrote the music for *The Sandbox* and *Malcolm*, brought him into contact with those who could offer some kind of critical appreciation of his work. W. H. Auden, for example, suggested somewhat pointedly that he should take up pornographic verse as a means of tempering his florid style, while Thornton Wilder, whom he met at the MacDowell Colony in Peterborough, New Hampshire, suggested that he should concentrate his attention on drama. In the next five years he produced nothing but poor poetry: but, after a period of severe depression, he gave up his job, and with his thirtieth birthday looming ominously he sat down to write a play. He himself explains: "I wrote 'The Zoo Story' on a wobbly table in the kitchen of the apartment I was living in at the time—at 238 West Fourth Street. I did a draft, made pencil revisions, and typed a second script, and that's the way I've been doing my plays since. I finished 'The Zoo Story' in three weeks. . . ."[17]

The Zoo Story was read by a number of New York producers and duly rejected by them all. Its subsequent progress towards eventual production has been detailed by Albee himself. "William Flanagan . . . looked at the play, liked it, and sent it to several friends of his, among them David Diamond, another American composer resident in Italy; Diamond liked the play and sent it on to a friend of *his*, a Swiss actor, Pinkas Braun; Braun liked the play, made a tape recording of it, playing both its roles, which he sent on to Mrs. Stefani Hunzinger, who heads the drama department of the S. Fischer Verlag, a large publishing house in Frankfurt. . . ."[18] Eventually it

[17] *Ibid.*
[18] "Preface", *The American Dream and The Zoo Story*, pp. 7-8.

received its first performance in Berlin, at the Schiller Theater Werkstatt, on 28 September 1959—some four months before its belated American debut at the Provincetown Playhouse.

In a way it is fitting that a play which attacks so directly the indifference and sterility of contemporary American life should have received its first performance in Europe. It is as though Albee's subversive nature had been instantly recognised by a theatre and a public of which he has become increasingly scornful. Certainly *The Zoo Story* sets the tone for most of his subsequent plays, for his subject here, as later, is America and what he takes to be its contempt for human values. All of his work indeed grows out of the belief, expressed by Henry Miller, that "Everything that was of beauty, significance or promise has been destroyed or buried in the avalanche of false progress".[19] To Albee, as, one fancies, to those other analysts of American decay Allan Ginsberg and Randall Jarrell, the zoo has suddenly become a horrifyingly accurate image of a society where furious activity serves only to mask an essential inertia and whose sociability conceals a fundamental isolation.

There is no disguising the heavily ironical tone adopted by the play's protagonist when he announces that he lives in "the greatest city in the world. Amen."[20] For his apartment, significantly, is in a crumbling house on Columbus Avenue, an address which itself indicates clearly enough the object of Albee's satire and the metaphorical basis of his work. But in the face of indifference and complacency Albee does not lapse into despair. He stresses the need for man to break out of his self-imposed isolation to make contact with his fellow man. What he is calling for, in other words, is a revival of love.

The necessity for the expression of this love, for a contact between human beings which is real, however repulsive

[19] Henry Miller, *The Air-Conditioned Nightmare* (London 1965), pp. 25, 27.   [20] *Z.S.*, p. 37.

or terrifying its expression may be, is expounded by Jerry, a "prophet" who comes from the West Side of New York City. His role as seer/Messiah emerges in the course of the play and climaxes with his eventual death, which is a sacrifice to redeem his fellow man.

The play opens as Jerry approaches a man who is reading a book on a bench in Central Park. The man, Peter, admits later that his reason for coming to this bench is its solitariness. It is a symbol of his isolation. Jerry, however, attempts, at first intellectually and then physically, to dislodge him from this bench. To Peter contact is synonymous with intrusion and such intrusion is to be rebuffed. Indeed, when Jerry strikes up a conversation, he is eager to avoid even this superficial rapport. The stage directions reveal him as "anxious to get back to his reading", "uncomfortable", and "anxious to dismiss him".[21] But when Jerry's insistence forces him to abandon the escapism of his book he decides to humour him by listening. It soon becomes apparent, though, that the stranger's questions are beginning to penetrate behind the placid exterior of this man whom Rose Zimbardo has correctly identified as the "modern version, in middle-class stereotype, of Everyman".[22] His marriage is revealed as an empty sham, to be regarded simply as a necessary asset for the successful man. As such, it has left him emasculated and finally alone. When Jerry's probing begins to reveal the basis of his failure of nerve in this way, Peter grasps at the first opportunity to reject the significance of his comments by dismissing him first as a beatnik from "the Village" and then as "mad". But Jerry resists these efforts to pigeon-hole him and realises that Peter is failing to understand or accept his message of the necessity for human contact. Accordingly he decides to simplify his message to the level of parable.

[21] *Z.S.*, pp. 12-13.
[22] Rose Zimbardo, "Symbolism and Naturalism in Edward Albee's *The Zoo Story*", *Twentieth Century Literature*, VIII (1962), p. 10.

He lives, he explains, in a large apartment building on the West Side in which the tenants are all outcasts of one kind or another. One is a coloured homosexual, another a Puerto Rican, and a third a solitary woman who cries all day behind a locked door. There is no contact between these tenants, and Jerry characterises it as a "humiliating excuse for a jail".[23] Thus, whether the image be that of a zoo or a jail, the bars which mark human isolation seem self-evident. It is against this background nevertheless that two attempts are made to establish contact with Jerry. The first of these takes the form of the sexual advances of his landlady and the second the physical attack of a dog which Jerry recounts to Peter in the form of a parable, "THE STORY OF JERRY AND THE DOG". In fact the landlady is so closely identified with the dog that it must be accepted that Albee intends them to be interchangeable, as symbols. For the dog, which is as hideous as its mistress, has a permanent erection which parallels the woman's sexual desire. It is also described as "making sounds in his throat like a woman",[24] while the landlady has eyes which "looked like the dog's eyes".[25] Both the dog and its mistress attack Jerry in the entrance to the building, a Freudian image which links violence to sexuality in a way which foreshadows *Who's Afraid of Virginia Woolf?* The symbolic nature of this story is further emphasised by an otherwise enigmatic statement which is, in effect, a perfect description of the process of symbolism. Jerry explains that "What I am going to tell you has something to do with how sometimes it's necessary to go a long distance out of the way in order to come back a short distance correctly".[26]

Jerry's response to these attempts to make contact is the same in both cases. He repulses them. He sees both the dog and the landlady as a threat to himself and as an invasion of the isolation which he has come to accept as

[23] *Z.S.*, p. 35.   [24] *Z.S.*, p. 31.
[25] *Z.S.*, p. 33.   [26] *Z.S.*, p. 30.

the norm of human existence. He offers the animal food
in an attempt to secure immunity from contact, and when
this fails he attempts to kill it. Although the dog survives
the poisoned food, it no longer attempts to make contact,
but lapses into the simulated indifference which, Albee
urges, is equally a mark of human relationships. It is at
this moment that Jerry suddenly reaches the understanding which sends him out in search of someone to
whom he can pass on his insight. For he realises that all
he has "gained" is "solitary free passage"[27]—continued
isolation. More important still, he recognises that the
dog's violence had indeed been an attempt to make
contact, and that, as such, it was an act of love: "We
neither love nor hurt because we do not try to reach each
other . . . was the dog's attempt to bite me *not* an act of
love? If we can so misunderstand, well then, why have
we invented the word love in the first place?"[28] It is this
message of the need for love in a world that places its
faith purely in appearances which Jerry carries with him
from the West Side; and it is, in effect, the ritual of
Jerry and the dog that is now acted out on the stage.
Peter now plays the role which Jerry had played in the
rooming-house, while Jerry plays the role of the dog. So,
too, Peter responds to Jerry's intrusion firstly by kindly
condescension, as Jerry had in offering the dog ham-
burger meat, and then finally by violence, as Jerry had in
attempting to kill the animal. Thus Jerry's description
of his own relationship with the dog could equally well
be applied to his relationship with Peter, and indeed the
normal state of human relationships before they have
been transformed by the gospel of love: "We regard each
other with a mixture of sadness and suspicion, and then
we feign indifference. We walk past each other safely; we
have an understanding."[29]

In a short story called "A Tree. A Rock. A Cloud",
Carson McCullers, whose *The Ballad of the Sad Café* Albee

[27] *Z.S.*, p. 35.   [28] *Z.S.*, p. 36.   [29] *Z.S.*, p. 35.

later adapted for the stage, describes the anguished attempts of an old man to outline his "science of love" to a young boy. He explains that love, human contact, is an art which has to be learned. One has to begin, he explains, with simple things, with a tree, a rock or a cloud. In his own case, he continues, "I bought a goldfish and I concentrated on the goldfish and I loved it. I graduated from one thing to another."[30] This science of love is essentially that which Jerry goes on to describe to Peter: "It's just that if you can't deal with people you have to make a start somewhere. WITH ANIMALS!... A person has to have some way of dealing with SOMETHING. If not with people ... SOMETHING. With a bed, with a cockroach ... with pornographic playing cards, with a strongbox...."[31] R. D. Laing, in considering the psychological plight of the isolated individual, has said that "The last hope of breakthrough ... may be through a homosexual attachment, or ... may be with the other as child or animal."[32] So it proves to be here, with Jerry realising the potential for communication "in an entrance hall ... with A DOG" and passing on his message to a man who petulantly claims to be a "GROWNUP", in a final consummation of contact which clearly has homosexual overtones.

Peter's response to the parable, however, is that of a man who can no longer find arguments, but who nevertheless still wants to cling desperately to his creed. He shouts out "I DON'T WANT TO HEAR ANY MORE"[33] and gets up to leave. In an effort to stop him, Jerry tickles him. This parody of contact, ironically, stimulates a momentary understanding on Peter's part of the nexus which Jerry has been trying to establish between the zoo and the nature of contemporary life. He even admits that "I had my own zoo there for the moment".[34] But Jerry

[30] Carson McCullers, *The Ballad of the Sad Café and other Stories* (Boston 1951), p. 138.   [31] *Z.S.*, p. 34.
[32] R. D. Laing, *The Divided Self* (London 1960), p. 159.
[33] *Z.S.*, p. 37.   [34] *Z.S.*, p. 39.

has decided to abandon his oblique approach in favour of explicit statement. He explains directly that "I went to the zoo to find out more about the way people exist with animals, and the way animals exist with each other, and with people too ... everyone separated by bars from everyone else".[35] He realises, however, that Peter is susceptible neither to allegory nor to direct persuasion. Accordingly he adopts the same strategy which the dog had used—violence. He provokes Peter into a defence of his bench—a mock battle in which he is seen absurdly defending the privacy and property rights which are clearly the basis of his values. But Jerry is determined that this violence will not revert to the casual indifference which had been the result of his encounter with the dog. Accordingly he throws a knife to Peter and then impales himself on it. Clearly contact has been established, for Peter is now inextricably tied to another human being, if only through a bond of guilt. The "middle-class" Everyman, then, has finally been released from the solitude which he had taken as a necessary and even desirable aspect of the human condition. As Jerry insists, he has been "dispossessed".

The symbolic force of the play's ending would appear to make nonsense of the suggestion, in a review of the play in *The Times Literary Supplement*, that Jerry's death is "an action of ultimate, futile contact".[36] For, as Rose Zimbardo has pointed out, the sacrifice which Jerry accepts as necessary is seen by Albee as being essentially a Christian one. Jerry is "crucified" so that Peter and his fellow men may be redeemed. When he accepts the need for sacrifice it is with the biblical expression of acceptance, "So be it".[37] He collapses onto the bench and in doing so changes its symbolic value from that of a refuge from human contact to that of the ultimate embracing of

[35] *Z.S.*, pp. 39-40.
[36] Anon, "Towards a Theatre of Cruelty", *T.L.S.* 27 Feb. 1964, p. 166.   [37] *Z.S.*, p. 47.

humanity—the Cross. The "wood and iron" of the
bench now gain an added significance. At the moment
of his "crucifixion" he cries out with a sound which Albee
insists must be "*the* sound of an infuriated and fatally
wounded animal",[38] thus uniting him in his sacrifice
with the dog/God from whom he had derived his message.
The man who had denied Jerry's message, as the biblical
Peter had denied Christ, now recognises him in the
triple affirmation which had marked Peter's return to a
real relationship with Christ and man. He replies to
Jerry's cry of "Peter ... Peter? ... Peter" with the
exclamation, "Oh my God ... Oh my God, oh my God."[39]

Jerry recognises this final conversion of his "disciple"
and confirms that his message has been passed on by
telling Peter that he has lost the vegetable quality of
indifference and has gained that mark of concern for
fellow man which has become associated with the potent
animal force. By wiping away the finger-prints on the
knife he absolves him from individual guilt for his
murder, as Christ had forgiven those who killed him
even as he was redeeming them. When Jerry directs his
disciple to take his book and go, it is clear that it loses its
former function as a symbol of isolation and becomes instead the new gospel of love.

The Zoo Story has, somewhat surprisingly, been seen by
many critics as a pessimistic play designed to demonstrate
the impossibility of human contact and the inevitability
of isolation. As such it has been presented as a natural
companion-piece to the works of Ionesco and Beckett.
Charles Lyons, for example, has said that "*The Zoo Story*
is within the genre classification of the absurd ... because
it assumes the absurdity, the chaos, of the human condition and its essential loneliness".[40] Even Gilbert

[38] *Ibid.*   [39] *Z.S.*, p. 48.
[40] Charles Lyons, "Two projections of the isolation of the human
soul: Brecht's *Im Dickicht der Staedte* and Albee's *The Zoo Story*",
Drama Survey, IV (1965), p. 13.

Debusscher, in an otherwise perceptive book on Albee, has said that "His theater belongs in the pessimistic, defeatist or nihilistic current which characterises the entire contemporary theatrical scene".[41] To accept this view and specifically to see in *The Zoo Story* only pessimism and nihilism seems to me little less than perverse. For, as we have seen, in this play the possibility of human dignity, the potential for meaningful sacrifice, and the viability of some kind of real contact are all established— a fact which is surely supported by the nature of the symbolism with which the playwright reinforces his message. Peter, at the end of the play, has been liberated from his false assumptions and is finally purged of his illusions. Never again, as Jerry insists, will he be able to retreat into solipsism; never again will he be able to repeat the frantic cry of the alienated and the disengaged, "leave me alone". Yet the fact remains that, following Martin Esslin's lead, critic after critic has tried to force Albee, willy-nilly, into the theatre of the absurd, thus forging a link between his scathing parables and the savagely ironical world of Samuel Beckett and Eugene Ionesco.

Albee, himself, perhaps only half-jokingly, has claimed that when he first heard the expression "theatre of the absurd", he automatically took it as a reference to Broadway. It is instructive, however, to note that the particular aspect of the absurd which he seizes upon as being of relevance to his own work is its insistence on the need to face reality. Here, indeed, is an undeniable point of contact. But the absurd implies more than this. It implies, as Esslin himself has pointed out, a world in which "man forever lonely, immured in the prison of his subjectivity" is "unable to reach his fellow man".[42] Here some kind of genuine distinction begins to emerge

[41] Gilbert Debusscher, *Edward Albee: Tradition and Renewal*, trans., A. D. Williams (Brussels 1967), p. 82.

[42] Martin Esslin, *The Theatre of the Absurd* (New York 1961), p. 293.

between Albee and the Europeans. To Beckett, man is not only trapped in his own subjectivity, but in a perverse way this solipsism is presented as the only possible reaction to the human situation. The boy in *Endgame* sits amid the ashes of the world contemplating his navel, while the protagonist of *Act Without Words 1* lapses into a state of total abstraction. Camus, too, who played a central role in defining the concept of absurdity, has Catherine offer the advice, in *Cross Purpose*, "Pray your God to harden you to stone. It's the happiness He has assigned Himself."[43] To Albee, as to Sartre before him, it is precisely this privatism which is to be deplored. Albee in fact places his faith in what Ignazio Silone has called the "absolute need for an opening on to the intimate reality of others"[44] —a concept which would have little meaning, except an ironical one, to Beckett. So it is that we can speak, without irony, of Albee's humanism and can seriously consider the "sainthood" of many of his characters. For, where Beckett emphasises the abandonment and absurdity of man in the face of an empty universe, Albee emphasises man's freedom. The difference between the two writers is essentially the difference between the determinist and the existentialist.

Ionesco has said: "I have no images of the world except those of evanescence and brutality, vanity and rage, nothingness or hideous, useless hatred . . . vain and sordid fury, cries suddenly stifled by silence, shadows engulfed forever in the night."[45] In revolt against what seemed to him to be the defeatism of this attitude, Kenneth Tynan launched his famous assault on Ionesco and the theatre of the absurd. He insisted that he personally was looking for "evidence of the artist who is not content with the passive role of a symptom, but

[43] Albert Camus, *Caligula and Cross Purpose*, tr. Stuart Gilbert (London 1965), p. 155.

[44] R. W. B. Lewis, *The Picaresque Saint* (London 1960), p. 110.

[45] *The Theatre of the Absurd*, p. 85.

concerns himself, from time to time, with such things as healing".[46] While this kind of statement tends rather to throw light on Tynan's own particular prejudices than to offer a constructive criticism of Ionesco's work, it does clarify the distinction between Ionesco and Albee, who in many respects has proved himself to qualify for Tynan's approbation. For if he has failed to embrace a strictly political dogma, he has formulated a positive response to the human predicament which rests on the ability of man to face reality with courage while working to establish genuine human relationships and real values.

Hence Esslin's casual inclusion of *The Zoo Story* in a recent Penguin called *Absurd Drama* has served merely to prolong a fundamental misunderstanding of its tone and purpose. For while Albee obviously owes a debt to certain European dramatists, namely Genet, Ionesco, and, perhaps, Dürrenmatt and Frisch, what is of greater interest is the manner in which he has adapted their style and dialectic to fit his own particular vision. To Albee solitariness is not an inescapable aspect of the human condition, but a strategy whereby the individual attempts to escape the consequences of freedom. The whole purpose of Jerry's parables and of his final sacrifice lies in his attempt to establish an unbreakable bond with the vacuous Peter, to make him commit himself to a relationship with another human being. He is intent on teaching him the truth of his assertion that "We have to know the effect of our actions".[47] The breakdown of communication which is apparent throughout most of the play derives not from some fundamental estrangement between man and his predicament but from man's fear of the reality which might be exposed by true lucidity. So it is that Peter is content to talk only so long as the discussion is limited to repeating opinions and phrases sanctioned by society and having no real meaning. It is when Jerry

[46] Eugene Ionesco, *Notes and Counter Notes*, tr. Donald Watson (London 1964), p. 100.   [47] *Z.S.*, p. 33.

becomes dangerously articulate, when he begins to expose with devastating accuracy the basis of Peter's compromise with existence, that Peter places his hands over his ears and refuses to hear any more. Communication is not impossible in Albee's world. It is simply avoided as being a threat to complacency and comfortable isolation. So it is that Albee's chief weapon as a dramatist, and perhaps the most significant gift which he has brought to the American theatre, is precisely this lucidity.

What is ultimately exposed by Jerry's calculated assault is precisely the failure of this archetypal member of the middle-class to seize on the essence of his humanity. Although by nature free, he surrenders his freedom to the group. He conforms in dress, in habits, and in thought. Although by nature able to communicate, he is prepared to sacrifice that very contact which could vitalise him. Essentially, therefore, Albee is attacking Peter's "bad faith". To Sartre this implied a willingness to concede the reality of a non-existent determinism. As Mary Warnock expresses it, it is "any denial that we can be other than we are. . . . It involves playing a role, and regarding our behaviour as determined by the role we play." Peter acts out the role of a member of the bourgeoisie, accepting effective emasculation as he had accepted the dictation of tastes and values. The obvious implication of Albee's play, as of Sartre's philosophical concept, is that man is ultimately free, "that even what role to play has originally been a matter of choice and that it remains a matter of choice whether to continue in that role or not".[48] When Peter leaves the stage at the end of the play, there can be little doubt that Jerry has succeeded in shattering the mask which has identified him as a *bona fide* member of American society but which has simultaneously served to obscure the humanity of his real face.

In this context, then, Wendell Harris's remark, in an

[48] Mary Warnock, *Ethics Since 1900* (London 1966), p. 125.

article in *Prairie Schooner*, that *The Zoo Story* is a brutal attack "on humanity itself"[49] seems more than a little wilful. Like Eric Mottram's observation that Albee is concerned with making "a serious comment on killing without false tragedy",[50] it seems disturbingly wide of the mark. But these assertions are indicative of the confusion which has surrounded both this and other of Albee's plays, a confusion deriving less from any direct ambiguity within the plays than from the bewilderment which invariably follows from an attempt to judge a playwright by outdated standards. Within the context of American drama Albee's work was something new. It introduced an idiom and a manner which could not be fitted into categories based on O'Neill, Williams, and Miller. Inevitably, therefore, criticism has lagged behind dramatic invention, and Albee has been castigated for faults he does not possess. Once it becomes possible to view him outside the context of the absurd, perhaps we shall be able to take another look at these early plays and recognise that Jerry, for example, is not an eccentric on the verge of suicide, as Wendell Harris suggests, but the first in a long line of Albee's protagonists who are capable of recognising the need to reject the cowardice of modern life and return to a faith in the efficacy of human contact in a world which if bleak need not be terrifying. To Albee, the Cartesian formula is an incomplete proof of existence, for Jerry's message is ultimately more meaningful. Albee accepts the definition formulated by Silone's Rocco in *A Handful of Blackberries*, "Amo ergo sum",[51] while, like the Italian novelist, he finds "in the human relation the seeds of a truly sacramental sensibility".[52]

[49] Wendell Harris, "Morality, Absurdity, and Albee", *Southwest Review*, XLIX (1964), 254.

[50] Eric Mottram, "The New American Wave", *Encore*, X (1964), p. 28.

[51] *The Picaresque Saint*, p. 175.

[52] *Op. cit.*, p. 29.

CHAPTER II

THE EARLY PLAYS II

Chekhov once pointed out that it is as profitable for a farmer to breed rats in a granary as it is for bourgeois society to nourish the artist—a thought which has no doubt occurred, in recent years, to those at the Valley Forge Military Academy who had sent Albee forth to "preserve America". Yet, for all his scathing criticism of American society, his work is dedicated to formulating genuine grounds on which such a preservation might be justified. If he seems to lack the kind of commitment which had typified the reformers of the nineteen-thirties, this is because he is concerned with a more fundamental sense of alienation than springs from merely social or political discontent. This is particularly true of his second play, *The Death of Bessie Smith*.

The idea for this play came to him as he was reading the notes on the sleeve of a record album of songs sung by the Negro blues-singer, Bessie Smith. Like *The Zoo Story*, this play, too, received its first performance in Germany, this time at the Schlosspark Theatre in Berlin.

In *The Death of Bessie Smith* Albee attempts to bring together a public and a private world, developing his two themes in alternate scenes. The first concerns the death of Bessie Smith herself; she died in 1937 from injuries sustained in a car-crash after being turned away from a white hospital ironically called Mercy Hospital. The second concerns the progressive deterioration of a white nurse who by the end of the play is as effectively destroyed on a spiritual level as is Bessie Smith on a physical one.

The nurse's father is a racist who attempts to escape his own insignificance by inventing a friendship with the town's mayor while reminiscing about a past glory which had never been his. She herself is as prejudiced and bitter as her father, but, unlike him, she is aware of a profound dissatisfaction at the core of her being. At work she deliberately taunts a Negro orderly who patiently accepts insults as the necessary price of assimilation. Her immediate frustration, however, derives from her relationship with a young white intern. For, although she is too alive to the "economic realities" to contemplate marriage at this stage in his career, she is flattered by his attentions and dreams of a future marriage. But her plans are threatened by his recalcitrant attitude towards the values which she, as a Southerner, endorses. He is a liberal, but for most of the play the nature of his liberalism is highly suspect, for, like the orderly, he is prepared to defer to the apparatus of power, even when that apparatus expresses itself through this woman. At the same time his commitment to the Loyalist cause in Spain never goes beyond a generalised interest, unless we can take his action in the play's final scene as evidence of a fundamental change of priorities. It is in this final scene, in fact, that the two main elements of the play are brought together and the private and public world are seen to be merely two aspects of the same thing. For in this final scene the Negro, Jack, arrives with the body of Bessie Smith and asks for help. Although the nurse wants to turn him away, the young intern agrees to help. With this act of compassion—useless, in so far as Bessie Smith herself is concerned, since she is already dead—he apparently succeeds in breaking free from a system to which he had previously submitted. At last human values assert themselves, and he evidently realises his freedom to act.

At the same moment the nurse recognises the extent of her own failure. For, if she is to remain faithful to her own prejudices, she has now to destroy the intern's career and thus her own chances of marriage. She becomes hysterical and begins to make a noise which Albee describes as "almost keening". But the "death" over which she laments is not that of Bessie Smith. It is the demise of her own chances and of the values in which she has always placed her faith. The play ends as the intern asserts his strength in a way which is reminiscent of Leroi Jones's play *Dutchman*. He strikes the hysterical girl; an act of violence which symbolises his newly discovered strength to fight against inertia.

Quite obviously this play contains all the elements of a bitter social, and even political, document. For not only is Bessie Smith effectively "murdered" by whites, but the hospital orderly, who bears the brunt of the nurse's abuse, confesses that his uncle had been run down and killed by a lorry full of state police while taking part in a Civil Rights demonstration. James Baldwin has already created a racial melodrama out of just such material in *Blues for Mr. Charlie*. But Albee never lets his play degenerate into a racial polemic, neither does he allow his metaphysical concern to be lost in the bitterness of immediate injustice. As Albee himself has said, " . . . while the incident itself, was brawling at me, and while the characters I had elected to carry the tale were wrestling it from me, I discovered I was, in fact, writing about something at the same time slightly removed from and more pertinent to what I had imagined".[1] His subject, therefore, is less the injustice provoked by race than the absurd spectacle of man's inhumanity to man; while his methodology depends on balancing the particular bitterness of the Southern situation against a more profound malaise which leaves the individual ambiguously poised between alienation and commitment.

The Death of Bessie Smith does not in fact represent the

[1] Edward Albee, *The Sandbox, The Death of Bessie Smith*, with *Fam and Yam* (New York 1963), p. 1.

abrupt change of direction which many critics have
suggested. Certainly the social element of Albee's work,
which was present in *The Zoo Story*, and which continues
through all of his later plays, is more directly evident
here. At the same time this does not amount to a purely
political statement. For the racial situation functions
here, rather as it does in Ralph Ellison's *Invisible Man*, as a
potent image of man's self-inflicted absurdity. Here, in a
concrete and immediate form, is that lack of compassion
which Albee sees as a mark of contemporary society.
Here, too, is that breakdown of communication, clearly
exacerbated by racial divisions, which he had already
noted in *The Zoo Story*. As in his first play, then, Albee is
primarily concerned with indicting a society which can
deny the urgency of human contact and compassion
while closing its eyes to an absurdity which is of its own
making. Like the nurse's father, virtually all of the
characters rely on some illusion to give their lives a sense
of purpose and have "a pretty hard time reconciling"
themselves "to things as they are".[2] The intern dreams of
a meaningful life in Spain, the orderly of becoming
successful in an integrated society. But, in order to
support these fantasies, they are forced to compromise
the values to which they pay lip service, and to support a
system which is ultimately dedicated to destroying those
very values. Although the nurse herself claims to be
"fully aware of what is true and what is not true",[3] she
conceives of reality purely in terms of power, money, and
practicality. Her pragmatic values thus lead her into a
similarly expedient submission to social injustice and
spiritual sterility. Unwilling to commit herself to genuine
human relationships, and caught out by her own
strategy of disengagement, she is forced, finally, into a
position of complete alienation. Aware briefly of the real
state of the world, she fails to opt for compassion, but
instead welcomes alienation as itself a final anodyne: "I

[2] *B.S.*, p. 54.   [3] *B.S.*, p. 57.

am sick of everything in this hot, stupid, fly-ridden *world*. I am sick of the disparity between things as they are, and as they should be! I am sick of the sight of *you* . . . I am sick of him . . . I am sick of talking to people on the phone . . . and I am sick of going to bed and I am sick of waking up . . . and I am tired of the truth . . . and I am tired of lying about the truth . . . I am tired of my skin . . . I WANT OUT!"[4]

The extent to which Albee is concerned with a fundamental sickness in American society rather than just a specifically Southern decadence is reflected, too, in the play's imagery. For much of the play is enacted against a back-drop of "a great, red-orange-yellow sunset".[5] This is a symbol of decay and apocalypse which clearly has implications beyond the immediate sphere of the South. For, while the intern himself recognises the symbolism and declares that "fire has enveloped half of the continent", he is also aware that "The West is burning".[6] So that, while many of the play's characters look to the North as offering a simple solution to their problems, Albee will accept no such simplicity. If the word "north" is repeatedly used virtually as a cabalistic incantation, it is clear that there can be no such easy solution. In the end, in fact, none of the characters escape to this mythical land of freedom, for, as Albee points out, we are living in a world in which "the panaceas don't work much any more".[7] The only hope for a society so precariously balanced on the edge of dissolution lies in the kind of fundamental "conversion" which had carried Jerry to the point of complete commitment. In *The Death of Bessie Smith*, however, the "conversion" remains ambiguous, for, although the intern sacrifices his "future" for a single act of compassion, his gesture is a quixotic one which fails to carry complete conviction. Nevertheless,

---

[4] *B.S.*, pp. 70-1.   [5] *B.S.*, p. 25.
[6] *B.S.*, p. 51.
[7] "Edward Albee Interviewed by Digby Diehl", p. 72.

for the first time a stand has been taken and the value of common humanity re-asserted.

While attacking society in general, Albee is undoubtedly more tolerant of his Negro characters. They alone demonstrate any warmth in personal relationships. They alone are identified by names instead of functions. The only exception to this rule is the orderly, who by the end of the play has become so closely identified with the white world which he envies that he, too, evidences its cruel indifference to suffering. Having seen Bessie's dead body, all he can say is: "I never heard of such a thing . . . bringing a dead woman here like that . . . I don't know what people can be thinking of sometimes. . . ." No wonder Albee's final stage direction indicates that the "great sunset blazes".[8] But, since the Negro characters fail to become anything more than vague sketches, the moral polarity which Albee implies lacks real justification. If we are supposed to see the orderly as evidence of the corrupting power of Western civilisation (a civilisation symbolised here by the mayor who lies impotently in hospital suffering from piles), then we can legitimately ask for a more convincing picture of his original humanity. Beneath Albee's subtlety there still seems to lurk the grinning stereotype of the happy-go-lucky, friendly Negro uncorrupted by the vices of the white man.

But for the most part *The Death of Bessie Smith* did contribute to Albee's growing reputation for powerful and original drama. If it was not the contribution to the Civil Rights dilemma which many critics thought it to be, it did nevertheless constitute another stage in Albee's examination of a decaying society. His main concern, however, was not with politics but with metaphysics; his main target not the racial bigot but the cynic. Thus a declaration made by the intern in the sixth scene can be taken as an accurate description not only of the theme of

[8] *B.S.*, p. 80.

this play but also of the faith which has animated Albee in all of his work from *The Zoo Story* to *A Delicate Balance*: "I am not concerned with politics . . . but I have a sense of urgency . . . a dislike of waste . . . stagnation."[9]

The first of Albee's plays to receive its premiere in America was a fourteen-minute sketch called *The Sandbox*. Having finished *The Death of Bessie Smith*, he was working on *The American Dream* when he was commissioned to write a short dramatic piece for the Festival of Two Worlds to be held in Spoleto, Italy. Albee has explained that, faced with this commission, he "extracted several of the characters from *The American Dream* and placed them in a situation different than, but related to their predicament in the longer play".[10] *The Sandbox* was not, in fact, performed at Spoleto, and finally received its first performance at the Jazz Gallery in New York on 15 April 1960, six days before the German premiere of *The Death of Bessie Smith*.

The play opens as an elderly couple, known simply as Mommy and Daddy, enter what is apparently a beach. An attractive young man is doing calisthenics beside a sandbox which serves as an image of this beach. They beckon for a musician to enter, and, as he plays, they go off stage to bring on Grandma, who is described by Albee as a "tiny, wizened woman with bright eyes".[11] She is carried on stage and placed in the sandbox, where she stays for the rest of the play. While Mommy and Daddy settle down to wait, Grandma describes her life directly to the audience. At her prompting, the stage lights fade; and, while Mommy and Daddy console one another with hollow protestations of concern, an off-stage rumble signifies her approaching death. The lights go off altogether, and, when they come on again, Grandma is seen partly buried in the sand. She pretends to be dead as

[9] *B.S.*, p. 59.
[10] "Preface", *The American Dream and The Zoo Story*, p. 9.
[11] *S.* p. 8.

Mommy and Daddy leave, content that they have shown the requisite concern and performed the necessary rites. But when Grándma tries to get up, she discovers that she cannot move. The Young Man crosses over to her and, like the ham actor he is, admits to being the Angel of Death. He kisses the old woman, and the play closes on this tableau with the Young Man bending over her.

The Sandbox is essentially an expressionistic glimpse at a society which resolutely ignores the message Jerry had given his life to communicate in *The Zoo Story*. For here human relationships are meaningless, and human affection has frozen into affectation. Mommy and Daddy, whose names alone signify the "vacuity of their characters",[12] are merely anxious to "do things well",[13] and, as they witness Grandma's death, they rattle off the clichés which reveal their crass insensitivity: "Our long night is over. We must put away our tears, take off our mourning . . . and face the future. It is our duty . . . it's hard to be sad . . . she looks . . . so happy."[14] Albee's play is, therefore, a direct attack on insincerity, euphemism, and sentimentality. It exposes the basic assumption of familial love as a sham, a pragmatic pose dictated by a society which values appearance above reality. Mommy and Daddy appear to show concern for Grandma, but this is less an expression of their humanity than of their sense of social obligation. Albee's satire, however, is directed not only against the inadequacies of a decadent society, but also against a theatre which itself condones these inadequacies. Like Pirandello before him, he is all too conscious of the inherent conservatism of the naturalistic theatre.

In the nineteen-twenties Pirandello rebelled against a theatre which called itself "realistic" while obscuring the essence of that reality behind empty rhetoric and sentimentality. He attacked, too, the process whereby theatrical devices had been allowed to harden into

[12] *S*. p. 8.   [13] *S*. p. 19.   [14] *S*. p. 18.

convention. But his protest went a good deal further than a sardonic comment on unimaginative production. For he was intensely aware of the falsity of a theatre which refused to face the brutal reality of the human condition. In *Six Characters in Search of an Author* one of his characters cries out in desperation at the theatre's distortion of life: "Of my nausea, of all the reasons . . . that have made this of me . . . you would like to make a sentimental romantic concoction."[15]

From Albee's point of view things had not changed a great deal by 1960, for then he diagnosed the crisis in the theatre as stemming from just such a lack of integrity and refusal "to face man's condition as it is".[16] He castigated particularly that audience which "primarily wants a reaffirmation of its values, wants to see the status quo, wants to be entertained rather than disturbed, wants to be comforted".[17] Clearly in this context *The Zoo Story* had been something of a declaration of intent, since it demonstrably succeeded in disturbing its audience, while retaining at its very centre just such a determination to face the human condition. It is *The Sandbox*, though, which represents his most direct expression of discontent with the naturalistic theatre. For, if he rejects an effete society, he rejects, too, a theatre which caters for it by enshrining its distorted values into art. When he deliberately stresses the theatricality of his play, he does so not in order to achieve a sense of clinical objectivity, but in order to expose the clichés of the theatre as he had those of society itself. His immediate tutor is Pirandello rather than Brecht. When a musician is hired to play during Grandma's death-scene and when the light grows

[15] Domenico Vittorini, *The Drama of Luigi Pirandello* (New York 1957), p. 298.

[16] Edward Albee, "Which Theatre is the Absurd One?", in John Gassner's *Directions in Modern Theatre and Drama* (New York 1965), p. 334.

[17] R. S. Stewart, "John Gielgud and Edward Albee Talk about the Theatre", *The Atlantic Monthly*, ccxv (1965), p. 65.

dim—after Grandma has prompted the electrician—
what we are witnessing are the formal clichés of death as
evidenced in the cinema and the naturalistic theatre.

Ironically, the play ends on a suspiciously maudlin
note, and it remains a moot point whether this represents
a conscious attempt to ridicule sentimentality, or
whether it is evidence of his own emotional involvement. But since the play is dedicated to his own grandmother, who had died only a short time before, the
somewhat mawkish ending seems more likely to have
been a concession to her memory than a conscious piece
of satire. Perhaps, too, it is for this reason that, despite its
faulty ending, Albee still considers this his favourite play.

The Sandbox is in some ways the closest that Albee has
ever come to producing an "absurd" play in the
European sense. Nevertheless there are clear indications
that his personal vision stops short of Beckett's nihilism.
For in the person of Grandma he creates a character
whose vitality and perception contrast directly with the
vacuity of those others who take part in her personal
endgame. She clearly has no patience with the hypocrisy
shown by Mommy and Daddy. She recognises their
clichés for what they are and in doing so surely suggests
the existence of other values. At the same time she faces
her death with a dignity and even a sense of touching
irony which seem to lift her above the immediate
absurdity of her situation. It is hard to think of any of
Beckett's characters of whom this could be said, for most
of them look to death as a welcome end to an absurd life
and yet remain incorrigible optimists in the face of the
most appalling bleakness. Nevertheless *The Sandbox* is
finally too brief a play to enable us to make any real
assessment of Albee's relationship to the absurd. In *The
American Dream*, on the other hand, the divergence
between Albee's and Beckett's particular visions becomes
more immediately evident.

While *The Sandbox* understandably provoked little

response from critics or public, his next play, *The American Dream*, attracted considerable attention. It opened off-Broadway at the York Playhouse together with a one-act opera, *Bartleby*, on which William Flanagan and Albee had collaborated. When this failed in production, it was replaced by *The Death of Bessie Smith*, so that for the first time it became possible to see a whole evening of Albee's work.

The American Dream is an expressionistic satire directed at contemporary American society. Albee has said that "it is a stand against the fiction that everything in this slipping land of ours is peachy keen". It "is a picture of our time—as I see it".[18] In *The Zoo Story* Peter had been forced to acknowledge the hollowness of his marriage and the emptiness of his personal life, but this had merely been a background against which Albee had projected Jerry's positive faith. With *The American Dream*, however, he concentrates more closely on the alternative to an authentic existence. He examines the basis of a society which is seemingly content to deprive itself of human values in order to inherit the dubious rewards promised by Horatio Alger Jr—wealth, security, and contentment.

At the very centre of his play Albee places that great symbol of American values—the family. As in *The Sandbox*, the mother and father are known only as Mommy and Daddy, names which, though sanctioned by the commercial sentimentality of Madison Avenue, clearly imply an element of immaturity while remaining ironically inappropriate to a play in which there is no place for the compassion and love which one would normally associate with parents. At the beginning of the play they exchange pointless platitudes in a conversation which has less to do with communication than with self-expression and which offers clear evidence of the woman's domination. For Mommy admits to having married her

[18] *A.D.*, p. 54.

husband simply for wealth and security and, having acquired both, wants no further contact with him.

The third member of the family is Grandma. As in *The Sandbox* she embodies the shrewd values of an earlier age. Indeed the essential conflict exposed by *The American Dream* is that between Grandma's innate compassion and insight and the heartless materialism of a new generation which has consistently sacrificed its humanity to a dream of success and material satisfaction.

Into this "family situation" there now comes a professional social worker, Mrs Barker, who, while uncertain as to the purpose of her visit, happily enacts the pointless rituals of social intercourse, even taking her dress off on the suggestion that she should make herself "comfortable". As the play progresses we learn that as a representative of the Bye Bye Adoption Service she had once "sold" Mommy and Daddy a young boy. When he had failed to give "satisfaction", Mommy had systematically mutilated him, destroying everything which signified his humanity. Evidently we are moving in a society in which the capitalist ethic has spilled over into the area of personal relationships, so that Mommy seriously demands the same satisfaction of people that she does of her other possessions.

This society is in fact typified by the Young Man who now enters in search of a job. He is a clean-cut "midwest farm boy type, almost insultingly good-looking in a typically American way".[19] Grandma immediately recognises him for what he clearly is—a personification of the American Dream. Like Kilroy and Chance Wayne, in Tennessee Williams' *Camino Real* and *Sweet Bird of Youth*, he is prepared to do anything for money, but like them, too, he is finally hollow. Indeed, when he confesses his own inadequacies, this serves also to underline the insufficiency of the society which he so accurately symbolises. For he admits that he is "unable to see any-

[19] *A.D.*, p. 107.

thing ... with pity, with affection ... with anything but ... cool disinterest ... I no longer have the capacity to feel anything. I have no emotions. I have been drained, torn assunder ... disemboweled. I have only my person ... my body, my face."[20] This macabre process of "dismantling", like that which Nathanael West describes in *A Cool Million*, is in effect Albee's account of the creation of modern American man—attractive, seductive, but totally devoid of human pity and compassion. When Mommy embraces this prodigy, at the end of the play, as a complete answer to her dream and as proof of the possibility of genuine satisfaction, this action, therefore, is merely an ironical comment on the true nature of that dream. The play closes as Mommy toasts the Young Man and Grandma steps out of the action, thus demonstrating the possiblity of dissent from a society which resolutely ignores reality in its passionate concern with appearance.

This, then, is Albee's nightmare vision of a loveless and hypocritical society in which people can legitimately be identified by their function, since they have long since surrendered their individuality. The villain of the piece is obviously Mommy—perhaps a covert expression of the strained relationship between Albee and his own foster mother as well as a generalised comment on Momism in the style of Kopit's *Oh Dad, Poor Dad*. She it is who professes love for the mother she is planning to commit to a home, while placing her faith wholeheartedly in a dream which is nothing more than a substitute for an authentic life. For the ambition which is the essence of this dream is revealed as a grotesquely unreal device for injecting meaning into an apparently purposeless existence—a process which Albee parodies in Daddy's desire to be a Governor rather than a Senator because "it would be nearer the apartment".[21] Against this vision of life is balanced only the perception of an old woman who alone is able to recognise the malaise of a society which fails to understand that "You got to have a sense of dignity 'cause, if you don't have that, civilization's doomed".[22]

As Gilbert Debusscher has pointed out, Albee's play can be seen as part of a continuing tradition of social and moral criticism in American drama. The idea of the American Dream itself had in fact provided the subject for Eugene O'Neill's *Marco Millions*, Clifford Odets' *Awake and Sing*, Arthur Miller's *Death of a Salesman*, and Tennessee Williams' *Camino Real*. But *The American Dream* has also been seen as a direct importation from an experimental European theatre. Debusscher calls it "Albee's frankest incursion into the Theatre of the Absurd",[23] while Esslin likewise sees it as a promising and brilliant "example of an American contribution to the Theatre of the Absurd".[24] Clearly there are points of contact between this play and, for example, Ionesco's *The Bald Prima Donna*. There is the same emphasis on the devaluation of language, the same contempt for bourgeois clichés and for that kind of conformity which finally destroys identity. Ultimately, though, the differences between the two plays are far more important than the similarities, for, as in *The Zoo Story*, Albee here accepts a potential for improvement which would have little meaning to either Beckett or Ionesco. For, when he says that his play is "an attack on the substitution of artificial for real values", he is, of course, assuming the existence of real values. When he adds that it is "a condemnation of complacency, cruelty, emasculation and vacuity",[25] he is indirectly implying a programme of his own.

Ionesco has said that "it is not any particular society that seems to me derisory. It is man."[26] *The Zoo Story* and

[22] *A.D.*, p. 64.
[23] Gilbert Debusscher, *Edward Albee: Tradition and Renewal*, p. 2.
[24] *Op. cit.*, p. 36.
[25] *The Theatre of the Absurd*, p. 227.
[26] Eugene Ionesco, *Notes and Counter Notes*, tr. Donald Watson (London 1964), p. 138.

The American Dream demonstrate just how fundamentally opposed Albee is to this viewpoint. For to him man, *per se*, far from being derisory, is capable of heroism and compassion. If a corrupt and intensely materialistic society is capable of provoking an absurd response, then Albee nevertheless continues to recognise the possibility of transcending this absurdity. In *The American Dream* the burden of his faith rests, as we have seen, on the character of Grandma, who represents a generation uninitiated in the torpid joys of consensus and group-therapy. Her calculated remarks establish her as a real alternative to a cruel and effete generation. She, as Albee had said of his own grandmother, is "outside the ring". Nevertheless, the fact that she is old, while not justifying despair, does underline the urgency of Albee's message. The positive act of dissociation which ends the play clearly indicates that dissent is a viable possibility, but the question still remains: are we capable of taking this step before comedy finally gives way to tragedy?

The originality of both *The Zoo Story* and *The American Dream* lies in the fact that while employing some of the techniques of the absurdists Albee has retained his own vision, which accepts neither the empty optimism of Broadway nor the complete nihilism of the absurd. His achievement, therefore, does not lie, as Esslin has suggested, in his ability to translate Ionesco's clichés into a distinctively American idiom, but in the skill with which he has rendered his own sense of the human spirit, which, in Lorraine Hansberry's words, "invariably hangs *between* despair and joy".[27] To Beckett's and Ionesco's characters he adds a crucial self-awareness which makes freedom a meaningful possibility and which establishes the existential basis of his work.

[27] Lorraine Hansberry, *The Sign in Sidney Brustein's Window* (New York 1965), p. lx.

CHAPTER III

WHO'S AFRAID OF VIRGINIA WOOLF?

Albee's excursion onto Broadway, in October 1962, brought him immediate success. For although *Who's Afraid of Virginia Woolf?*, his first full-length play, was denied the Pulitzer Prize (two members of the drama committee resigning in protest), it did receive both the New York Drama Critics' and Tony Awards for the best play of the 1962-3 season. While running for two years on Broadway it also appeared with great success in most European capitals—in Prague, somewhat intriguingly, under the title *Who's Afraid of Franz Kafka?*

In some ways, this considerable success was a potential source of embarrassment to a former doyen of off-Broadway, for from the standpoint of the non-commercial theatre financial success was all too frequently allied to aesthetic compromise. Certainly Diana Trilling, writing of *Who's Afraid of Virginia Woolf?* in her *Claremont Essays*, saw just such a direct relationship between the play's popularity and what she took to be its consequent shallowness. While this kind of schematic criticism seems to hold a certain persuasiveness when applied to a dramatist who has always been highly critical of mass taste, Albee has pointed out with considerable justice that the "popularity of a piece of writing will always tell you more about the state of critical letters and public taste than it will about the excellence of the work".[1] Certainly an attempt was made to bring to the commercial theatre some of the values and personnel of off-

[1] Edward Albee, "Creativity and Commitment", *The Saturday Review*, 4 Jun. 1966, p. 26.

Broadway. The play was produced by Richard Barr and Clinton Wilder, who had worked with Albee on his earlier plays, and together they made a conscious effort to avoid the usual excesses of Broadway production, even producing it for less than half the cost of a normal production.

The play is ostensibly a Strindbergian sexual drama set in a small New England college. George is a professor of history and his wife, Martha, the daughter of the college president. At the beginning of the play, having returned from a party, they entertain Nick, a new lecturer in biology, and his wife Honey. As the night wears on, the liquor seems to provoke them into a ritual of violence and abuse which gradually draws in their guests, and which rapidly reveals the inadequacy of their lives. But, for all the virulence of their battles, it is not until Martha breaks a private agreement and mentions the existence of a son that the "games" of the first act take on a more serious aspect. In the second act, indeed, spurred on by George's pose of indifference, Nick and Martha attempt to commit adultery, an act of calculated sensuality which finally forces George to act. Accordingly he deliberately sets out to exorcise those illusions behind which they have all been sheltering. He forces Nick and Honey to acknowledge the emptiness of their marriage, while consciously destroying the illusory child with which he and Martha had compensated for their own sterility. The play ends as Honey faces her fear of sexuality and George and Martha hesitantly face a future without protective illusions.

Despite Daniel MacDonald's suggestion, in an article in *Renascence*, that the play is about the "necessity of illusion",[2] an interpretation supported by the prestigious *Tulane Drama Review*, *Who's Afraid of Virginia Woolf?* is in fact centrally concerned with the need to abandon

[2] Daniel MacDonald, "Truth and Illusion in *Who's Afraid of Virginia Woolf?*", *Renascence*, XVII (1964), 63.

fantasy in order to return to a real relationship with one's fellow man. It is an attempt to penetrate beneath the appearance of modern society to get down to "the bone ... the marrow".[3] Its original title, *The Exorcism*, is therefore an apt description both of the play's central theme and of Albee's method. If its present title seems a little bewildering, we have Albee's assurance that it was originally derived from a slogan which he had once seen scrawled on a mirror in a Greenwich Village Bar and that it means "who's afraid of life without false illusions?"[4] The three acts, "Fun and Games", "Walpurgisnacht", and "The Exorcism", thus represent three stages in Albee's careful dissection of a society which clings to fantasy under the impression that it is essential to survival. For to Albee, as to Karl Jaspers, "Man cannot evade this situation. ... He might tranquillise himself in the self-forgetful pleasures of life. ... But one day iron reality would again confront him."[5] This is a precise description of the action of Albee's play, which, like Jasper's book, is concerned with the plight of man in the modern age.

The first act brings together the two couples, the younger a carbon-copy of the older. The difference between them lies purely in the skill with which George and Martha have learnt to mask their sterility and the degree to which they have purposely allowed reality and illusion to mingle. Hence while George and Nick are ostensibly contrasted, on a deeper level they are painfully alike. In their separate ways they both represent forms of escapism. As George admits, "When people can't abide things as they are, when they can't abide the present they do one of two things ... either they turn to a contemplation of the past, as I have done, or they set

[3] *V.W.*, p. 125.

[4] William Flanagan, "Edward Albee: An Interview", *The Paris Review*, XXXIX (1966), p. 103.

[5] Karl Jaspers, *Man in the Modern Age*, tr. Eden and Cedar Paul (London 1951), p. 194.

about to ... alter the future!"[6] George, the historian, looks to the past both as protection from reality and as a welcome escape from conformism. An intellectual, his intellect is directed, for the most part, into sterile argument which gives him the illusion of vitality and positive existence. Yet underneath this delusive animation, he remains impotent and his life pointless.

Nick, the scientist, whose name was reportedly intended as a reference to the totalitarianism of Nikita Khrushchev, represents the "wave of the future". His values are purely those of the American Dream. He is confident of inevitable success and shows himself ready to adapt his morality to the demands of expediency. A biologist, he is attacked by George for the Huxley-like world which he is intent on creating and which he, in part, represents. In essence he is but another version of the Young Man in the *American Dream*. Despite his attractive appearance, he too proves to be impotent, as, George insists, will be those generations to be created, not out of human intercourse, but out of the synthetic products of science. For science, as well as presenting a positive threat, is to Albee just another form of Faustian distraction in a play whose Faustian overtones are repeatedly emphasised. This, as Nietzsche had said, is "Science as self-anaesthetic".[7] For Albee, then, the only genuine response to present reality, for society as for individuals, is direct confrontation. To him the advice offered by the charlatan Dr Tamkin, in Saul Bellow's *Seize the Day*, contains genuine perception: "The real universe. That's the present moment. The past is no good to us. The future is full of anxiety. Only the present is real—the here-and-now. Seize the day."[8]

In this act, too, we are given an insight into the tech-

[6] *V.W.*, pp. 106-7.
[7] Quoted in H. J. Blackham, *Six Existentialist Thinkers* (London 1953), p. 28.
[8] Saul Bellow, *Seize the Day* (New York 1956), p. 66.

nique whereby George and Martha insulate themselves
from the immediate reality of their situation. For the
mock battles and "games" which they engage in are in
fact their attempt to simulate some kind of meaningful
activity. Like the protagonist of Dostoyevsky's *Notes from
Underground*, they feel that "we can at least lacerate
ourselves from time to time, which does liven us up a bit
... it's better than nothing".[9] George, therefore, is
telling the strict and literal truth when he describes
their battles as "walking what's left of our wits",[10] and
Martha is almost as accurate when she suggests that
George is attracted to her precisely because of her
ability to maintain the pressure of her insults. For the
games have indeed replaced genuine contact, and the
excitement which they generate is a substitute for sexual
fulfilment, as well as an alternative to a real existence.
Perhaps also they offer proof of the validity of Dr Hendrik
Ruitenbeek's comment that "paradoxically, it often
seems that only in conflict can a person in the alienated
middle-class experience 'the other' as an existential
reality".[11]

Like Beckett's Vladimir and Estragon, George and
Martha refuse to pass up any opportunity for distraction.
In fact their frenzied bouts are little more than articulate
equivalents of the slapstick episodes in *Waiting for Godot*,
while the scene in which George and Martha exchange
insults ("Monstre!/Cochon!/Bête!/Canaille!/Putain!")
has a direct equivalent in Beckett's play ("Moron!/
Vermin!/Abortion!/Morpion!/Sewer-rat!").[12] In a real
way, therefore, Albee's play is an attack on a highly
articulate but essentially absurd society which substitutes "sad games" for a real life lived with courage and

[9] Fyodor Dostoyevsky, *Notes from Underground*, tr. Andrew R.
MacAndrew (New York, 1961), p. 118.

[10] *V.W.*, p. 27.

[11] Dr Hendrik Ruitenbeek, *The Individual and the Crowd: A Study of
Identity in America* (New York 1965), p. 92.

[12] Samuel Beckett, *Waiting for Godot* (London 1959), p. 75.

compassion. In sketching out his own ideas on absurdity, Albert Camus himself had in fact devised a schematic representation of just such a situation; a diagram which matches exactly the circumstances of *Who's Afraid of Virginia Woolf?*

Absurdity   Lucidity[13]

| |

Games without Consequences

The second act, "Walpurgisnacht", appropriately emphasises those further Faustian distractions—drink and sexuality. Certainly liquor has played its part in George and Martha's retreat from reality, and George's remark that "We drink a great deal in this country, and I suspect that we'll be drinking a great deal more too . . . if we survive"[14] establishes a direct connexion between the plight of this middle-aged couple and the society which they represent. But clearly such a casual resort to opiates has its own dangers. For the child whom George and Martha have created is used instead as a weapon in a way which is at first reminiscent of Strindberg. In *The Dance of Death*, for example, the similarly dominant wife, Alice, points out that "What should have been the uniting link became the seed of dissension; what is held the blessing of the home turned into a curse".[15] To Strindberg, though, the scramble for the child's affection was merely objective proof of the evils of marriage, while to Albee it is proof of the inadequacy of illusion. For, far from acting as a consolation, the fantasy child serves rather to exacerbate their plight and isolate them still further from the real contact which they so desperately need. At its most extreme moreover this kind

[13] Albert Camus, *Carnets 1935-1942*, tr. Philip Thody (London 1963), p. 5.
[14] *V.W.*, p. 67.
[15] August Strindberg, *Eight Famous plays*, tr. Edwin Björkman and N. Erichsen (London 1949), p. 341.

of withdrawal seems to be closely allied to insanity, for all four of his characters frequently lapse into a child-like behaviour and language which George specifically identifies as an aspect of madness, for the insane "don't grow old. . . . They maintain a firm-skinned serenity . . . the under-use of everything leaves them quite whole."[16] This is a point which Albee reinforces by means of a cautionary story. George describes a young boy who, unable to face the guilt and isolation which follows his accidental killing of his parents, is placed in an asylum. Here he is cut off from a world which horrifies him but is thereby alienated from the human contact which is, to Albee, the essence of salvation. The suspended animation of this boy who has "a needle jammed in his arm" thus becomes an accurate image of a society which similarly finds reality too much to face without the protection of alcohol and fantasy. The relevance of this parable to George's own situation is underlined by Martha's insistence that George, too, had killed his parents in precisely the manner which he had ascribed to the young boy.

Towards the end of the second act, the "fun and games" become more caustic, and under George's relentless probing we begin to penetrate to the truth. The real nature of Nick and Honey's marriage is laid bare, and Honey is for a moment shocked into admitting her fear of human contact. Even George himself is provoked into renouncing an illusory world.

In the third act George consciously destroys the remaining illusions. As Martha rehearses the detailed mythology with which they have given substance to their fantasy child, he chants the Latin of the burial service. Having broken the rules of the game, Martha now has to accept the "death" of her "son" as final. But, as the exorcism draws to an end, there is evidence that genuine human contact has again become a possibility.

[16] *V.W.*, p. 63.

Honey now wants to have a child, while George and Martha admit for the first time that they are equally responsible for their sterility—an admission which Albee, in a stage direction, significantly sees as evidence of a new sense of unity; a unity which is itself emphasised by the tableau with which the play ends. George and Martha embrace and admit their fear of reality as George quietly sings the song which is the play's title. The implied optimism of this ending has earned the play the ironical but nonetheless accurate title of *Long Night's Journey into Day*—a title which became more literally correct with the film version, whose closing shot was of George and Martha seen against a background of the dawning day.

In *The Last Analysis* Saul Bellow had propounded a similar notion of man's instinctual response to frustration and fear, and in doing so precisely identified the various stages of withdrawal through which George and Martha pass in Albee's play. For to Bellow, man, "Cut off by self-pity. Passivity. Fear. Masochistic rage", retreats into "Delusion. Intoxication. Ecstacy. And Comedy."[17] As we have seen, delusion, intoxication, and the frenetic pursuit of ecstasy all play their part in anaesthetising those unwilling to face the real world. Comedy, however, has a more ambiguous function in Albee's play than it does in Bellow's. For *Who's Afraid of Virginia Woolf?* shows evidence of that blend of comedy and anguish which one associates more particularly with Pirandello or Beckett, whom Albee has called the "one living playwright I admire without any reservation whatsoever".[18] Henri Bergson, in his classic essay, saw the function of laughter as lying in its ability to "intimidate by humiliating",[19] and there is little doubt that Albee

[17] Saul Bellow, *The Last Analysis* (New York 1965), pp. 71, 78.
[18] "Edward Albee: An Interview", p. 106.
[19] Henri Bergson, *Laughter*, tr. C. Brereton and F. Rothwell (London 1911), p. 198.

uses humour essentially as a weapon, as a means of stripping his characters of false dignity and pretension. But the humour of *Who's Afraid of Virginia Woolf?* also has another function. It operates, rather as does Mark Twain's humour in *Huckleberry Finn*, as a means of tempering an unpalatable truth. For in the context of New Carthage, laughter, as Bellow had suggested, can be as much of a retreat as sex or liquor. The young boy who had killed his parents retreats into manic laughter, while Honey hides her fear behind a simulated amusement. In a sense the audience too is coerced into sharing this form of escapism. With George and Martha it feels a temporary exhilaration, only subsequently to realise, with them, the bitter reality masked by the humour. This is an essential aspect of Albee's declared intention to "corrupt" the audience "in the direction of the truth".[20] Humour, then, for Albee is both the sugar-coating and the chief active ingredient of the pill in a play whose method is based on what Dostoyevsky once called "joking between clenched teeth".[21]

To Albee, therefore, to retreat from reality, whether into delusion or comedy, is to retreat also from one's humanity. While Eugene O'Neill, like Ibsen before him, had insisted that to deprive man of his illusions was ultimately to undermine his sanity, and even to destroy his life, Albee rejects this message and continues to insist that "in the long run" it is "best for people to try to live with the truth".[22] Perhaps it is possible even to detect an ironical comment on O'Neill's stance in the play itself when Martha adopts an Irish brogue to parody the typically O'Neill sentiment, "Awww, 'tis the refuge we take when the unreality of the world weighs too heavy on our tiny heads".[23] This kind of retreat is evidently

---

[20] "Edward Albee interviewed by Digby Diehl", p. 65.
[21] *Notes from Underground*, p. 115.
[22] Lee Baxandall, "The Theatre of Edward Albee", *Tulane Drama Review*, IX (1965), p. 33.   [23] *V.W.*, p. 111.

seen by Albee as a failure of nerve which can only
serve to produce men like Nick or the Young Man of
The American Dream—the empty men of whom Eliot had
written in "Burnt Norton", who "Cannot bear very
much reality" and who are

> Distracted from distraction by distraction
> Filled with fancies and empty of meaning
> Tumid apathy with no concentration.[24]

In the world described by Albee contact is by no
means impossible. It is quite simply avoided. Honey
literally runs away from it, while her husband preserves
a "scientific detachment in the face of life"[25], responding
to George's attempt to "communicate" with a contemp-
tuous "Up Yours!"[26] As Harold Pinter has said of
contemporary society, "instead of any inability to
communicate there is a deliberate evasion of communication".[27] If this society is an "absurd" one, it is so
because of its distorted values and not because of the
hopelessness of its situation. This distinction, as we saw
earlier, is a crucial one, for Albee has said that the
problem is to understand whether human beings are as
they are because they must be or because they want to
be. Writers like Beckett and O'Neill identify a strict
determinism which, if it relieves man of responsibility,
denies also the possibility of any improvement. To Albee,
however, this interpretation of the human condition is
too restrictive. Where O'Neill had been concerned with
establishing a compromise between the individual and
his situation, and where Beckett presents a vision of that
individual overwhelmed by his situation, Albee discovers
genuine hope. For he sees in the confrontation of reality
the first step towards a genuine affirmation, which lies
not through "pipe-dreams" (as it did for O'Neill in *The*

[24] T. S. Eliot, *Collected Poems 1909-1935* (London 1958), pp. 186,
188.   [25] *V.W.*, p. 64.   [26] *V.W.*, p. 73.
[27] *The Theatre of the Absurd*, p. 207.

Iceman Cometh), but through a positive acceptance of human limitations and of the need for real human contact. To avoid reality, then, is to invite disaster. The boy in George's story who swerves to avoid a porcupine succeeds only in crashing into a tree.

The possibility of meaningful action thus lies at the very centre of Albee's personal philosophy, for he has described the artist's central responsibility as resting in his ability to describe accurately the world he sees and to say "Do you like it? If you don't like it change it."[28] If this means that he accepts man's freedom to influence his surroundings, it also suggests that to Albee the writer has a social role to play. It is hardly surprising, therefore, to find him saying that "the responsibility of the writer is to be a sort of demonic social critic".[29] This is a point, too, which is especially worth remembering when considering *Who's Afraid of Virginia Woolf?*, which, as indicated earlier, is all too often regarded simply as a Strindbergian drama of sexual conflict.

The relationship between Albee and Strindberg has been stressed by a number of critics, and there are certainly demonstrable parallels between *Who's Afraid of Virginia Woolf?* and, for example, *The Father*, *The Bond*, and *The Dance of Death*. Indeed, despite Albee's avowals to the contrary, the bitterness with which he approaches his female characters is so like Strindberg's that one is hardly surprised to find that certain speeches are virtually interchangeable. When Laura in *The Father* says to her husband, "Now you have fulfilled your destiny as a father and family supporter—a function that unfortunately is a necessary one. You are no longer needed . . .",[30] one recalls not only the central image of *The American Dream* but also the misogamy of *The Zoo Story*. At the same time the captain's speech in the same play provides an even more precise parallel to the essential

[28] "Edward Albee Interviewed by Digby Diehl", p. 72.
[29] *Op. cit.*, p. 72.   [30] *Eight Famous Plays*, p. 41.

situation of George and Martha in *Who's Afraid of Virginia Woolf?*: "We too—as so many others in the world—have lived our lives unconsciously, like children, full of fanciful conceits and notions, ideals and illusions, until at last we woke up."[31]

Despite the seductive precision of these parallels, it would clearly be misleading to consider Albee simply as an American Strindberg whose chief value lies only in his ability to modernise the battle of the sexes. For, to Albee, the breakdown in the relationship between husband and wife is indicative of a more fundamental failure in communication, while the impotence of the male is a particularly accurate symbol of what he takes to be the sterility of the contemporary world. His real subject, then, is not marriage but society; his real aim human contact and not sexual reconciliation, and his real enemy illusion and not feminine dominance.

Indeed when George plays his game of "Get the Guests", he prefaces his story with a warning which could equally well be applied to the play itself. He insists that "it's an allegory, really—probably—but it can be read as straight cozy prose".[32] When Albee adds that "George and Martha may represent the Washingtons, and the play may be all about the decline of the West",[33] far from throwing out a red herring he is directing our attention to one of the play's central themes. For Albee has himself pointed out that "there is contained in the play . . . an attempt to examine the success or failure of American revolutionary principles".[34]

The setting for the play is the township of New Carthage—a name which is itself a comment on the society which it contains. St Augustine, in settling in Carthage, a city whose success had contained the seeds of its own destruction, had confessed, "to Carthage I

[31] *Op. cit.*, p. 40.   [32] *V.W.*, p. 86.
[33] "Albee: Odd Man in on Broadway", p. 50.
[34] "Edward Albee: An Interview", p. 110.

came, where there sang all around me in my ears a cauldron of unholy loves".[35] In *The Waste Land* T. S. Eliot derives from this same remark in the *Confessions* a sense of the false standards of a sterile society in which personal values had become degraded. So Albee's play, set in a Carthage of the New World, is similarly dedicated to an insistence on the falsity of the values adhered to by that society. In this atmosphere personal relationships are corrupted to serving material ends, and, as in *The Zoo Story* and *The American Dream*, marriage itself is degraded. Martha confesses that her motives for marrying were influenced by pragmatic politics; she wanted to marry into the college. So, too, Nick admits that his marriage had stemmed, not out of any real relationship between himself and Honey, but rather out of the necessity created by her hysterical pregnancy and the fact of her considerable fortune. For all the savagery between Martha and George and Nick and Honey, therefore, *Who's Afraid of Virginia Woolf?* is by no means simply concerned with personal antagonisms. As in his earlier plays, Albee is concerned with a more general inadequacy arising out of man's failure to establish a meaningful relationship between himself and his situation.

Thus, although *Who's Afraid of Virginia Woolf?* appears to lack the overtly social dimension of *The Death of Bessie Smith*, it does in fact embody the essence of Albee's social dialectic. He himself has said: "we are no longer looking for panaceas against all evils or solutions manufactured abroad. Our aim is to prevent our political system from being denatured by too much facile conformism.... This," he adds, "is already a programme in itself."[36] This is no petulant complaint against the consensus, but rather a desperate attempt to arrest the decay of a modern society which, like that pictured in *The American Dream*,

[35] Augustine, *The Confessions of St Augustine*, tr. E. D. Pusey, (Oxford 1938), p. 29.
[36] "Towards a Theatre of Cruelty", *T.L.S.*, 27 Feb. 1964, p. 166.

increasingly values appearance above reality and conformity above individuality. So George, the defeated liberal who has largely opted out of a world whose values he does not share, becomes a crucial figure in the Albee canon. It is he who represents the dilemma of the modern individual in a world in which "Accommodation, adjustment, malleability . . . seem to be the order of things".[37] For all his desire to defend the irrational, the rebel, the artist, and perhaps even the deviate, he himself has given way to the pressures of society. He has accepted a putative reality because it is easier and apparently more comfortable to do so. But Karl Jaspers has insisted that "The reality of the world cannot be evaded", pointing out that "Experience of the harshness of the real is the only way by which a man can come to his own self".[38] It is precisely George's initial failure to face the "reality of the world" which gives a literal truth to Martha's description of him as "a blank, a cipher . . . a zero".[39] But, like Jerry and Peter in *The Zoo Story*, he is finally provoked into fighting for a genuine life. He is made to acknowledge a commitment which goes beyond an intellectual loyalty to the democratic spirit.

The alternative to this revival of personal commitment is made painfully obvious. As Nick and Martha attempt to commit adultery in the kitchen, George reads from a book the Spenglerian prophecy that "the west must . . . eventually fall",[40] while he himself likens the significantly named New Carthage to those other devastated cities, Gomorrah and Penguin Island (Anatole France's mythic island destroyed by its own inhuman capitalism). Indeed it is interesting to note that Spengler himself drew a parallel between Carthage and modern America, while indicting both the commercialism and the sterility of modern man, even going so far as to suggest that in this climate of sterile intellectualism "Children do not

[37] *V.W.*, p. 65. [38] *Man in the Modern Age*, p. 178.
[39] *V.W.*, p. 18. [40] *V.W.*, p. 104.

happen . . . because intelligence at the peak of intensity can no longer find any reason for their existence".[41] The repeated references to sterility and destruction in fact establish an apocalyptic alternative which has an immediate relevance in the era of the Cold War, while Albee's desperate warning has the foreboding ring of a Catonian prophecy.

Yet we must surely feel at the end of the play that some kind of viable alternative has been formulated. For George no longer feels the need to retreat into the past, and Honey no longer sublimates her fear of a brutal reality in her parallel refusal to stomach food. At the same time, Martha is finally released from the dubious refuge of her illusions. So, as the day begins to break, they are all finally reduced to what Pirandello has called "naked figures", with the promise, surely, that a new and more genuine life is possible both for these individuals and for the society of which they are an essential part. As Jaspers says in describing what he himself sees as the single hope for man in modern society, for "the individual, thrust back into his own nudity, the only option today is to make a fresh start in conjunction with the other individuals with whom he can enter into a royal alliance".[42] Just such a "royal alliance" is clearly mirrored in the tentative and almost innocent contact with which George and Martha close the play. They cling together, freely admitting their fear, but no longer sublimating that fear in fantasies or hiding their sense of isolation behind a barrage of language. Hence at the end of the play, the dialogue becomes for the first time drastically simplified as contact is established at a more meaningful level. The violent rhythm and splendid articulateness of the linguistic battles give way to a slow and simple dialogue which mirrors the uncomplicated state to which their relationship has returned:

[41] Oswald Spengler, *The Decline of the West*, tr. C. F. Atkinson (London 1926-8), ii, p. 104.   [42] *Man in the Modern Age*, p. 194.

GEORGE [*Long silence*]. It will be better.
MARTHA [*Long silence*]. I don't . . . know.
GEORGE. It will be . . . maybe.
MARTHA. I'm . . . not . . . sure.
GEORGE. No.
MARTHA. Just . . . us?
GEORGE. Yes.[43]

Albee's first full-length play is, therefore, what George calls "a survival kit", proffered to an audience which Albee sees as living in a threatened New Carthage blissfully unaware of its own inadequacies and of the urgency of a return to genuine human values.

Who's Afraid of Virginia Woolf? has been generally hailed as a significant return to naturalism. In an article in the *Bucknell Review*, Emil Roy saw it as being in "the naturalistic mainstream of Williams and O'Neill"[44]; and Tom Driver, in *The Reporter*, remarked that "*Who's Afraid* . . . is supposedly a realistic depiction of how life is".[45] But Albee is obviously not trying to produce simply a realistic slice of life. As Alan Schneider, the play's Broadway director, has pointed out, "We certainly never thought of it as being realistic" in the sense of attempting "a literal view of life in 1964 on a particular campus". Even the apparently realistic setting is intended to have a metaphorical force, for Schneider has emphasised that Albee wanted "the image of a womb or a cave, some confinement".[46] If the play was to be called realistic, Albee insisted that it would be necessary to re-define the term to mean that drama which faces "man's condition as it is"[47]; a description which

[43] *V.W.*, pp. 139-40.
[44] Emil Roy, "*Who's Afraid of Virginia Woolf?* and the Tradition", *Bucknell Review*, XIII (March 1965), p. 29.
[45] Tom Driver, "What's the Matter with Edward Albee?", *The Reporter*, 2 Jan. 1964, p. 38.
[46] Alan Schneider, "Reality is not enough", *Tulane Drama Review*, IX, (1965), p. 146.
[47] "Which Theatre is the Absurd One?", pp. 334-5.

effectively defines the role of the dramatist in a society
intent only on distraction and entertainment.

The success of *Who's Afraid of Virginia Woolf?* continued
in 1966-7 with the award-winning film version, starring
Richard Burton and Elizabeth Taylor and directed by
Mike Nichols. To those who, like Albee himself, "assumed
they would get Doris Day in it, and maybe Rock
Hudson",[48] the end result was surprisingly impressive,
primarily, one suspects, because it remained so faithful
to the text. Several small cuts were made as a gesture to
propriety—one cut delightfully serving only to make an
innuendo more starkly apparent—and only some twenty-
five words were added by Ernest Lehman, who was
credited with the screenplay. These additional words
were made necessary by the inclusion of the roadhouse
scene—a break with the play which was both unnecessary
and largely regrettable, since it destroyed the sense of
confinement at which Albee had specifically aimed. The
one major fault which the film did demonstrate was a
tendency to emphasise the emotional at the expense of
the intellectual, so that Elizabeth Taylor's description of
the film as a "love story" was a deal more accurate than
it should have been. Nevertheless, the aggressive sexuality
with which she played the part of Martha may have
served to expose the inanity of one commonplace of
Albee-criticism. For it had been widely reported that the
play was actually about four homosexuals disguised as
heterosexual men and women. Remarkable as it may
seem, this interpretation was widely canvassed and, one
supposes, credited. Yet there is little or no internal evidence to support such an interpretation; and Albee
himself has said emphatically that the play "was written
about two heterosexual couples. If I had wanted to
write a play about four homosexuals, I would have done
so."[49] This kind of fundamental misunderstanding has
dogged Albee since *The Zoo Story* was first dismissed by

48 "Edward Albee: An Interview", p. 100.   49 *Op. cit.*, p. 103.

one critic as a parable directed to proving that the pederasts will inherit the earth.

To many critics, from the Boston city censor to the editor of the *Tulane Drama Review*, the play appeared morbid and pessimistic, while Albee was merely concerned with exercising his acknowledged talent for bitter invective. To Harold Clurman, for example, "The right to pessimism has to be earned within the terms one sets up. The pessimism and rage of *Who's Afraid of Virginia Woolf?* are immature."[50] Perhaps, though, it is worth recalling what John Galsworthy had to say on this subject, for he pointed out that "the optimist appears to be he who cannot bear the world as it is, and is forced by his nature to picture as it it ought to be, and the pessimist one who cannot only bear the world as it is, but loves it well enough to draw it faithfully".[51] It is clear also that, while Albee's play attacks the false optimism and myopic confidence of modern society, it does ultimately affirm the existence of other values. In an existential sense it reaffirms the possibility of choice and the reality of freedom.

Like Virginia Woolf, Albee believes that there is a "need for the writer to capture the reality of his age."[52] In fact it may be worth quoting the end of Virginia Woolf's *Between the Acts* for the light it throws on Albee's play and perhaps also on the title itself. For in talking of a married couple who have grown apart she says, "Before they slept, they must fight; after they had fought, they would embrace. From that embrace, another life might be born. But first they must fight, as the dog fox fights with the vixen, in the heart of darkness, in the fields of night. . . . The house had lost its shelter."[53] This seems a fair description of the

---

[50] Harold Clurman, "Theatre", *The Nation*, 27 Oct. 1962, p. 274.

[51] John Galsworthy, "Some Platitudes Concerning Drama," in *Playwrights on Playwriting*, ed. Toby Cole (London 1960), p. 47.

[52] Mark Goldman, "Virginia Woolf and E. M. Forster: A Critical Dialogue", *Texas Studies in Literature and Language*, VII (Winter 1966), p. 388.   [53] Virginia Woolf, *Between the Acts* (London 1941), pp. 255-6.

situation which exists at the end of Albee's play. The house is no longer a shelter, or, as Albee has said, "a womb or a cave". George and Martha are forced to face reality, but are allowed also to come together for the first time in the play.

CHAPTER IV

TINY ALICE

With *Who's Afraid of Virginia Woolf?* Albee's reputation seemed assured. He was rapidly promoted into the official hierarchy of American culture, being granted the instant canonisation which is increasingly a mark of the American critical scene. Not only did he take on the conventional role of lecturer and literary arbiter, but he also played his part in spreading the good news of native enlightenment. At the behest of the State Department, he and John Steinbeck were enrolled as literary ambassadors and took part in a cultural exchange programme with various countries in eastern Europe (a gesture which did not prevent *Izvestia* launching an attack on his "modernism" in July 1967). In the autumn of 1964 he participated in a conference of Pan-American writers held in the Bahamas.

At home the success of his Broadway *début* made it possible for him to do something to help other young American playwrights. With some of the profits from *Who's Afraid of Virginia Woolf?* he established a theatre workshop, Playwrights 66, while, together with Clinton Wilder and Richard Barr, he helped to finance productions by new writers at the Cherry Lane Theatre, off-Broadway. His own work, however, inevitably suffered from a comparison with his first major success. Certainly none of his subsequent plays has received the same popular and critical acclaim. His adaptation of Carson McCullers' *The Ballad of the Sad Café*, which opened a year after *Who's Afraid of Virginia Woolf?* and which is discussed in the next chapter, was coolly received, and

Tiny Alice, which followed in December 1964, confused and confounded critics and public alike. Nevertheless, it was immediately apparent that he remained fundamentally dedicated to the principles of off-Broadway, resolutely refusing to repeat the formula which had already brought him such success and choosing instead to experiment with substance and form. The resultant disaffection of critics and public left him, if not unmoved, at least unrepentant, and he indulged in one of those fruitless duels with the press which Arthur Miller had waged a few years before.

The central idea for *Tiny Alice* came to Albee as he was reading a newspaper account of a man who had been kept imprisoned inside a room which was itself inside another room. Something about this "Chinese-box" situation appealed to him both because of its relevance to the problems of dramatic structure and because of the fascinating metaphysical aspects which these contingent realities suggested.

When the play first appeared in New York, its reception was something less than ecstatic. At best it was thought to be a personal therapy paralleled perhaps by Tennessee Williams' *Camino Real*; at worst it was a confidence trick pulled on the world in general and the drama critics in particular. When the dust had begun to settle and the play was published, Albee's bland assurance, in an author's note, that the meaning of the play was so clear as to obviate comment did little to convince those who had been completely baffled by the performance itself. Neither did it serve to redeem a work which unquestionably remains more effective in print than on the stage.

The play opens in a garden as a Cardinal and a lawyer discuss a billion-dollar grant which Miss Alice, a young but apparently eccentric semi-recluse, wishes to make to the Church. An implied condition of this grant, it seems, is that the Cardinal's secretary, a lay-brother called Julian, shall be sent to arrange the final details. In his eagerness to concur, the Cardinal is obviously prepared if necessary, to sacrifice not only his secretary, but also his dignity and principles.

When Julian goes to the castle in which Miss Alice lives, it becomes apparent that she, in conjunction with the lawyer and her butler, is part of a conspiracy aimed at seducing him away from the Church. But, in the place of spiritual commitment, they offer him only reality, an uncompromising and unattractive alternative to one who has sheltered behind expansive illusions. For the world with which they confront him is a restrictive place in which the individual is cut off from any final consolation and forced to create his own meaning and identity. Although Julian eventually marries Alice he refuses to accept the "tiny" world for which she is the surrogate. The conspirators are thus forced to shoot him and leave him to discover the truth of their precepts as he faces his death.

If the need to face reality was the main principle which emerged from *Who's Afraid of Virginia Woolf?*, then Albee had done little to define exactly what he meant by reality in that play. He had made no attempt to integrate the metaphysical world into his picture or to assess its validity as a part of the reality to which he urged his characters. With *Tiny Alice* he remedies this and attempts to analyse the whole question of religious faith.

Nevertheless, there is a direct connexion between *Tiny Alice* and *Who's Afraid of Virginia Woolf?*, between brother Julian's religious reveries and George and Martha's frenetic distractions. For when Albee stresses the relationship between spiritual ecstasy and erotic satisfaction, as he does by emphasising the sensuous nature of Julian's visions, he is not intent simply on making a cheap debating point about the nature of evangelical power. His thesis is rather that the individual craves a spiritual distraction just as he craves a carnal one—as a substitute for a frightening reality. Just as Nick had turned to sexuality as a retreat from the real world, so Julian turns to religion for much the same reason. Where George had created a fantasy son to fill a vacuum in his own life, Julian "creates" a son of God.

Indeed Albee is at pains to point out that Julian's early religious conversion had stemmed, not from a sudden sense of mystical enlightenment, but from fear. Afraid to face the implications of a world which seemed both empty and pointless, he had abdicated his responsibility by positing the existence of a god—a process which Albee elaborates in some detail. Julian describes the frightening situation of a person who finds himself locked inside an attic closet. In order to retain sanity that person is forced to assume the existence of somebody who can eventually open the door and release him. To Julian this is an apt description of his own "conversion", for, as he admits, "My faith and my sanity . . . are one and the same."[1] The need to personify this abstraction leads logically enough to a belief in God. In another story/ parable Julian describes the moment in his childhood when he had first felt the need to create this abstract "saviour". He explains that, after he had been severely injured in a fall, his calls for help had gone unanswered. Gradually his call had changed from an appeal to his grandfather to a plea to God, whose non-appearance is accountable, and who is the personification of the need to be helped. Thus for Julian the abstract world clearly represents an apparent compensation for the inadequacies of the temporal world and man's fear of loneliness. It is interesting to note just how closely this explanation of religious conversion matches that given by Alain Robbe-Grillet in an essay entitled "Nature, Humanism, Tragedy". He sees this process, though, as an arrogant extension of humanism by which the individual seeks to exaggerate his significance. While Albee would reject this

[1] *T.A.*, p. 45.

particular interpretation, he nonetheless clearly shares his belief that this strategy represents an inauthentic response to life. "I call out. No one answers me. Instead of concluding that there is no one there . . . I decide to act as if someone were there, but a someone who, for one reason or another, refuses to answer. The silence that follows my outcry is hence no longer a true silence, it is now enhanced with content, with depth of meaning, with a soul—which sends me back at once to my own soul . . . my hope and my anguish then confer meaning on my life . . . My solitude . . . is transformed at last by my failing mind into a higher necessity, into a promise of redemption."[2] But, as Robbe-Grillet goes on to warn, if this is "a path towards a metaphysical 'beyond,' " it is also "a door closed against any realistic future"; for if "tragedy consoles us today, it also forbids all more solid conquests for tomorrow".[3]

For all Julian's desire to believe in an after-life which will grant some kind of retrospective meaning to the real world, he is unable to place his faith wholeheartedly in this man-made God. Indeed it is this element of doubt, the fact that he remains fundamentally "dedicated to the reality of things, rather than their appearance",[4] which at one stage had taken him to an asylum, his faith temporarily lost, and which makes him an ideal subject for the conspiracy. For the conspirators sense that he is "walking on the edge of an abyss, but is balancing. Can be pushed . . . over, back to the asylum/ . . . Or over . . . to the Truth."[5] The truth with which they confront him is the need, in Alice's words, to "accept what's real".[6]

But this is precisely the crucial question: just what is "real"? Is reality simply the limited world of human possibilities in which death provides an apparent proof of futility, or is it the more expansive world in which

[2] Cited by Herbert Kohl, *The Age of Complexity* (New York 1965), p. 233.   [3] *Op. cit.*, p. 234.
[4] *T.A.*, p. 138.   [5] *T.A.*, p. 106.   [6] *T.A.*, p. 167.

"faith is knowledge"[7] and the individual an element in a grand design? Who is right, the existentialist or the determinist, the secularist or the Christian? Should Julian place his faith in God, "Predestination, fate . . . accident",[8] or should he embrace the restricted world of human suffering and love?

Distrusting language, as he had in *The Zoo Story* and *Who's Afraid of Virginia Woolf?*, Albee chooses to dramatise this dilemma in symbolic terms. The central symbol which he uses is that of a "model" castle which dominates most of the play. This "model" seems to be an exact replica of the castle within which the action takes place. It is accurate in every detail. When a fire breaks out in the larger castle it also breaks out in the "model". But Julian is uncertain in which of the two it had originated, and therefore uncertain as to which is the original and which the copy. This Platonic paradox clearly lies at the very heart of the play, as it does of Julian's crisis of conscience. For he remains unsure of the true nature of reality until the very end of the play, when he is converted, as Martin Buber would say, "to this world and this life".[9] In symbolic terms, this is represented by his acceptance of the "model" castle as the "real" one and the larger version as merely a projection of it—an interpretation which the lawyer himself endorses when he says of the castle in which he lives that "it *is* a replica . . . Of that . . . [*Pointing to the model*]".[10] The conspiracy, therefore, is evidently devoted to convincing Julian that he should accept this apparent diminution of his concept of reality. As the lawyer advises him, "Don't personify the abstraction, Julian, limit it, demean it".[11]

While Plato's idea of the real world clearly differed in

[7] *T.A.*, p. 165.   [8] *T.A.*, p. 160.
[9] Rev. James Richmond, *Martin Buber* (Nottingham 1966), p. 13. The text of a lecture delivered at Nottingham University on 17 Mar. 1966.   [10] *T.A.*, p. 85.   [11] *T.A.*, p. 107.

kind from Albee's, one feels that they would both concur in Plato's belief that the function of knowledge is "to know the truth about reality".[12] Indeed, the sort of trauma which faces Julian when he is urged to accept the apparently diminutive "model "as symbolising reality is comparable to that which faced Plato's man in the cave. For the world of reality is, almost by definition, unattractive to those who have lived sufficiently long with illusion. It is precisely for this reason, in fact, that the conspirators are forced to employ a more acceptable image of the real world in the person of Alice.

Miss Alice is herself identifiable with the "model" castle, which is actually referred to by the conspirators as "Alice"—a name which itself means "truth". She is a surrogate, a fact which she explains to Julian in a confession which can also be taken as Albee's justification for his resort to metaphor, "I have tried to be . . . her. No; I have tried to be . . . what I thought she might, what might make you happy, what you might use, as a . . . what? . . . We must . . . represent, draw pictures, reduce or enlarge to . . . to what we can understand."[13] Thus, if Julian cannot accept the God of society, the conspirators are prepared to offer him a "true" God. For the Butler insists that there "is *some*thing. There is a 'true' God." It is the Lawyer, however, who explicitly identifies it: "There is Alice, Julian. That can be understood. Only the mouse in the model. Just that."[14]

In the moments before his death Julian comes finally to recognise the inversion of his values which has resulted from his contact with Alice. For as he looks at a phreno-logical head, which Albee has rather pointedly left on stage throughout most of the play, he realises that his compulsion has always been to grant reality only to abstractions; to see man, in other words, solely in terms of this head with its eyes focused on some far horizon (the

[12] Plato, *The Republic of Plato*, tr. F. M. Cornford (London 1955), p. 180.   [13] *T.A.*, p. 161.   [14] *T.A.*, p. 107.

afterlife) rather than as a creature of flesh and blood
existing in a concrete world.

> Is that the ... awful humour? Art thou the true arms,
> when the warm flesh I touched ... rested against,
> was ... nothing? ... Is thy stare the true look? ...
> The ABSTRACT ... REAL? THE REST? ... FALSE? It
> is what I have wanted, have insisted on. Have nagged
> ... for. IS THIS MY PRIESTHOOD, THEN? THIS WORLD?"[15]

Julian himself, for whom abstention from intimate
human contact has been a sworn article of faith, is left
finally reconciled to the fact that his priesthood is indeed
in this world and that its whole object lies in making
contact with the "warm flesh" of his fellow men.

Julian's death is pointedly a crucifixion, a martyrdom
enacted against the model castle which is the epitome of
reality and truth. Indeed one ending, later discarded,
would have left him actually tied to the model. As he
dies, in a reversal of his former "conversion", his cry to
God now changes to a cry for Alice. At the same time
his mind reverts to the image of the person shut up in
the attic closet, and he admits, what he would not have
admitted before, that "No one will come".[16] (In the
original ending this closing scene was actually to have
been played inside a closet—an idea which finally had to
bow to theatrical practicality.) Julian also, arrives at a
further realisation, one that might be taken both as
the reason for his own retreat into illusion and as an
explanation of Albee's own obsessive insistence on the
necessity of violence. He comes to understand that
"Consciousness ... is pain".[17]

As Julian dies, the heartbeats which had reverberated
with an increasing intensity suddenly cease as well—an
audible confirmation that ultimately man is indeed his
own God and the only supra-reality that which he creates
himself. The secular evangelism of the conspirators has

[15] *T.A.*, pp. 188-9.   [16] *T.A.*, p. 176.   [17] *T.A.*, p. 181.

thus created its own saint in Julian, and they leave after covering the furniture with sheets in a way which is clearly intended to suggest the veiled images of Holy Week. Like Jerry before him, Julian has accepted a sacrifice which provides the basis for a new religion of man, which, if it grants no reality to metaphysical abstraction, does at least define the limits of human activity. For Albee clearly believes, with the novelist Ignazio Silone, that "The first sign of manhood is a shedding of abstractions in an effort to press toward 'an intimate opening on to the reality of others' ".[18]

If the symbolic pattern of *Tiny Alice* is essentially Platonic, the dilemma which that pattern highlights is, as Albee has shown in his previous plays, one central to modern society. It is interesting to see, in fact, just how closely Julian matches the archetypal neurotic in retreat from reality as outlined by a pioneer in psychology, Alfred Adler. The very precision of this parallel, indeed, tends to grant to Albee's creation the general application which is clearly his aim. Adler terms escapism "Safe-guarding through distance". His description of the neurotic fits Julian's situation precisely. His reference to the past, his concern with death, and his choice of religion are all recognised by Adler as symptoms of this desire to "safeguard through distance".

> To think about the past is an unobtrusive, and there-fore popular, means of shirking. Also, fear of death or disease. . . . The consolation of religion with the hereafter can have the same effect, by making a person see his actual goal only in the hereafter and the existence on earth as a very superfluous endeavour. . . .[19]

An American psychiatrist, Dr Abraham Franzblau, reminds us that Freud himself had felt that religious

[18] R. W. B. Lewis, *The Picaresque Saint* (London 1960), p. 151.
[19] Alfred Adler, *The Individual Psychology of Alfred Adler*, ed. H. L. Ansbacher and R. R. Ansbacher (London 1958), p. 277.

dogma stemmed ultimately "from man's unwillingness to accept mortality, to recognize the rapacious cruelty of nature, or to sacrifice some of his libidinous gratifications for the help he needs from his fellow men".[20]

The title of Albee's play would seem to suggest that *The Collected Works of Lewis Carroll* should be necessary reading, and several critics have in fact been at pains to insist on its relevance. For clearly Alice's Wonderland, as an escape from "dull reality", can be seen as a parallel to Julian's wonderland of religion, in so far as it grows out of a similar unwillingness to accept the restrictions of reality. Moreover, the confrontation of reality and illusion, which lies at the heart of Albee's play, is achieved in Carroll with a symbol which, like Albee's, is essentially Platonic. But while Carroll's literally "tiny" Alice is a part of the illusory world, Albee's tiny Alice symbolises reality. If Carroll insists on returning his protagonist to the real world at the end of his book, it is, perhaps, not without a nostalgic glance back over his shoulder to his wonderland, however brutal that wonderland may at times appear. There is no such nostalgic glance in Albee.

Julian has to relinquish the abstraction which is his retreat from reality. In doing so he abandons the robes of the Church for the clothes of ordinary life, a change which symbolises his shift of identity. This assumption of identity as a function of an adopted role is reminiscent of Nigel Dennis's satire on the great abstractions of modern society, *Cards of Identity* (1956). Here, too, three conspirators effect a change of identity in a man lured to their "mansion" by the prospect of monetary gain—a change signified here, as in *Tiny Alice*, by a physical change of clothes. To Dennis, also, religion is one of those projections whereby man escapes from the immediate reality of his situation and accepts a ready-made

[20] A. N. Franzblau, "A Psychiatrist Looks at 'Tiny Alice'", *Saturday Review*, 30 Jan. 1965, p. 39.

identity. It is an escape, moreover, which implies a denial of intellect, as it does a denial of reality. In Dennis's ironical words, "God is worshipped as a solid only by backward people; once educated, the mind reaches out for what cannot be grasped, recognises only what cannot be seen: sophistry adores a vacuum"[21]; or, more succinctly, as he puts it in his unabashed satire on religion, *The Making of Moo* (1957), "You have nothing to lose but your brains".[22]

Once again, however, the writer whose work offers the closest parallel to Albee's is T. S. Eliot. In a real sense *Tiny Alice* can be seen as a prose version of *The Cocktail Party*. In this play Eliot had presented a similar conspiracy of three designed to "save", in this case, four people. Like Julian, these characters are

> stripped naked to their souls
> And can choose, whether to put on proper costumes
> Or huddle quickly into new disguises.[23]

Edward and Lavinia, who form the nucleus of an involved romantic tangle, choose to retreat into just such a disguise. Having been confronted with the real world, they reconcile themselves to their situation in a way which brings them to the verge of indifference. They

> Learn to avoid excessive expectation,
> Become tolerant of themselves and others
> Giving and taking, in the usual actions
> What there is to give and take. They do not repine;
> Are contented with the morning that separates
> And with the evening that brings together
> For casual talk before the fire
> Two people who do not understand each other

[21] Nigel Dennis, *Two Plays and a Preface* (London 1958), p. 7.
[22] *Op. cit.*, p. 194.
[23] T. S. Eliot, *Collected Plays* (London 1962), p. 193.

Breeding children whom they do not understand
and who will never understand them.[24]

Eliot is at pains to draw a clear distinction between this
kind of soulless reconciliation and a genuine decision to
face the fundamental reality of the human condition in
order to construct some kind of meaningful response to it.
Edward's mistress, Celia, does just this. She realises that
she has been living in an essentially unreal world and
comes to understand, as does Julian in Albee's play, that
her version of reality has been

only a projection
. . . of something that I wanted—No, not *wanted*
—something I aspired to—
Something that I desperately wanted to exist.[25]

If she comes now to accept the stark horror of a world in
which communication seems impossible, in which
"everyone's alone,"[26] in doing so she also discovers her
responsibility to love. It is this perception which sets
her on a path leading directly to her crucifixion—a
fitting climax to the life of an individual whose values
differ so fundamentally from those of society. When
Julian faces his "crucifixion", it is with a similar understanding of the true nature of reality and of the need to
acknowledge a commitment to his fellow man. In both
cases the decision is celebrated by the conspirators with
a champagne toast in a sacrificial gesture in keeping
with this martyrdom.

In *Tiny Alice*, therefore, Albee's apocalyptic vision,
implied in *Who's Afraid of Virginia Woolf?*, is more clearly
defined. The abstract fear of the former play is crystal-
lised in Julian's perception of the terrifying loneliness of
man. Used to the projections of his own sensibilities, he
has to come to accept a diminution of his concept of reality.

---

[24] *Op. cit.*, p. 189.   [25] *Op. cit.*, p. 154.   [26] *Op. cit.*, p. 186.

He also has to accept his responsibility for creating his own identity and meaning. For Albee is insisting that man's freedom and identity ultimately depend on his ability to discount reliance on an abstraction which is the creation of his own metaphysical solitude. As Goetz had said in Sartre's *Lucifer and the Lord* (1951), "God is the loneliness of man. . . . If God exists, man is nothing".[27]

Albee has said that "the new theatre in the United States is going to concern itself with the re-evaluation of the nature of reality and, therefore, it's going to move away from the naturalistic tradition".[28] *Tiny Alice*, like *Who's Afraid of Virginia Woolf?* before it, is proof of Albee's personal devotion to this principle. Indeed, when Alice makes her first appearance dressed as an old crone, only to throw off her disguise and appear in her full beauty, this in itself is surely an indication of Albee's central purpose in a play which he himself has called "a morality play about truth and illusion",[29] and which is clearly dedicated to stripping the masks from religion, hypocrisy, materialism, and cant.

Albee is concerned, then, with what Thomas Mann, in a slightly different sense, has called the "dark under-side" of man, those areas in his life, that is, which he tries desperately to conceal even from himself. For Albee, like Pirandello and later Genet, is all too aware of the internal and external pressures on the individual to escape from doubt, ambiguity, and uncertainty by retreating into a pre-determined role—whether that role be shaped by the Church or by society. For as a clearly defined functionary man feels that he is no longer adrift in a purposeless world, but is part of what he is prepared to accept as a meaningful order. Albee is

[27] Jean-Paul Sartre, *Lucifer and the Lord*, tr. Kitty Black (London 1952), p. 133.

[28] Digby Diehl, "Edward Albee Interviewed by Digby Diehl", *Transatlantic Review*, No. 13 (Summer 1963), p. 62.

[29] Thomas B. Markus, "Tiny Alice and Tragic Catharsis", *Educational Theatre Journal*, XVII, p. 230.

finally concerned with this individual's response to seeing himself without a mask. He is concerned with penetrating behind the façade of public assurance to the true sense of fear, desertion, and real courage which he sees as lying at the heart of the human predicament. This, in a sense, is that "dissolution of the ego" which Joseph Wood Krutch has seen as the essential subject of contemporary literature. To Albee, though, it is essential to dismantle the ego, not in order to find the source of its psychosis, but rather to discover the foundation of its strength. Like the protagonist of Ralph Ellison's *Invisible Man*, Julian has to dive down into the depths of his consciousness before he can emerge again with a valid response to his surroundings.

But this is essentially an internalised drama—one which is of necessity acted out within the mind of the protagonist. This in itself accounts for Albee's move here towards monologue. For when Albee describes *Tiny Alice* as "something small enclosed in something else",[30] he is not only referring to the central symbol of the castle, but also to the structure of a play which can be legitimately seen as a monodrama taking place entirely within Julian's own tormented mind. To the extent that this is true, a great deal of the obscurity and ambiguity which lies at the heart of the play can be seen as a direct expression of Julian's own bewilderment—a fact which nevertheless fails to redeem the confusions of a play which all too often substitutes technical facility for genuine engagement. Where Pirandello had succeeded in translating his metaphysical conundrums into flesh and blood, *Tiny Alice* remains for the most part a merely ingenious exercise. Pirandello justifiably boasted that he had converted the intellect into passion. In the place of passion Albee offers only refined anguish.

In *Who's Afraid of Virginia Woolf?* Albee had attempted

[30] Lee Baxandall, "The Theatre of Edward Albee", *Tulane Drama Review* IX (1965), p. 36.

to communicate beneath the level of language by creating a sub-structure of imagery. In *Tiny Alice*, his precise control of this imagery ultimately breaks down, and instead of operating as an endemic part of the play, as did the fantasy child in his former play, it becomes little more than a substitute for dramatic action. Indeed, Albee becomes every bit as inept as Tennessee Williams, who has always had a penchant for littering his stage with any number of highly significant objects, from dried up fountains and anatomical charts to iguanas. While the castle probably represents a high-point in mishandled symbolism, perhaps the single most painful symbol is the phrenological head which is left on stage for most of the play, apparently so that Julian may remark on it in the final scene. One effect of this rather gross mishandling of imagery was that audiences tended to be thrown into varying degrees of confusion; and, while reviewers responded to its obvious power and originality, they likewise found its meaning somewhat elusive. Further, Albee's admission, in the author's note which precedes the published play, that "*Tiny Alice* is less opaque in reading than it would be in any single viewing", is an incredible confession for a dramatist to make. For in choosing to write for the theatre he has presumably accepted the challenge of communicating directly to an audience, and in this he has patently failed. He is, it appears, clearly not prepared to make any concessions to the audience—not even those made necessary by the nature of drama.

His failure in *Tiny Alice*, moreover, makes one doubt what is clearly one of the play's central premises. For the assumption that the model is more "real" than the castle itself has a further implication. It implies that art itself is more valid than an inauthentic life founded on nothing more secure than fear and illusion. In the rarefied atmosphere of *Tiny Alice*, one is far from convinced.

In his own defence Albee has suggested that an audience might require several visits in order to fathom the play's various depths. Unfortunately this is not borne out by the experience of one man. John Gielgud, who played Julian, found that time did not make the play any more comprehensible for him. Perhaps, therefore, there was more than a little truth in the answer which Albee offered to Gielgud's incomprehension: "I know you want to know what the play's about, John, but I don't know yet, so I can't say."[31]

[31] R. S. Stewart, "John Gielgud and Edward Albee Talk about the Theatre", *Atlantic Monthly*, CCXV (1965), pp. 67-8.

CHAPTER V

TWO ADAPTATIONS:
THE BALLAD OF THE SAD CAFÉ
AND
MALCOLM

Both Edward Albee and the Georgia-born authoress Carson McCullers started life with one ambition. They wanted to be concert pianists. Mrs McCullers' musical career ended abruptly when she lost her tuition money in the subway, while Albee's scarcely got off the ground owing to his inability to play the piano. When the two finally met, it was not, however, to discuss their musical failings, but to consider Albee's somewhat disappointing adaptation of Carson McCullers' *The Ballad of the Sad Café*, which opened on Broadway on 30 October 1963.

That Albee should choose to follow the extraordinarily successful *Who's Afraid of Virginia Woolf?* with an adaptation is in itself somewhat surprising, since he distrusts such adaptations and on one occasion told an interviewer that "there is a tendency to cheapen—to lessen the work that's adapted". Nevertheless, he admitted at the same time that from the moment he had first read Mrs McCullers' novella, in 1952, he had felt that "If I ever start writing plays I'd like to make this into a play", because "it seemed to me to belong on the stage." But obviously his interest goes considerably beyond a desire to find out "if it is possible to do an adaptation of somebody else's work".[1] For while *The Ballad of the Sad*

[1] Digby Diehl, "Edward Albee Interviewed by Digby Diehl", *Transatlantic Review*, 13 (Summer 1963), p. 57.

Café is an expression of Carson McCullers' own particular vision, it also represents a logical extension of Albee's thematic concerns as revealed in the earlier plays. It demonstrates, too, a continuing sense of affinity with some of the perceptions of the absurdists. For the absurd is not a purely European invention, and Albee clearly sees in the grotesque distortions of Southern literature images every bit as relevant and accurate as Beckett's Pozzo and Ionesco's Amédée. The view of human isolation accepted by these "American absurdists" is no less terrifying than that accepted by their European counterparts, but almost invariably they formulate a viable response to that nameless terror either in the frenzied power of primitive religion (Flannery O'Conner), or in an insistence on the endurance of the land (Faulkner) and the power of love and the human spirit (McCullers). It is this fact which attracts Albee to the violent parables of Carson McCullers and later to the equally violent images of James Purdy, a Mid-Westerner who, like Sherwood Anderson before him, shares the Southern concern with the grotesque. While these writers do share certain assumptions with writers like Kafka, Beckett, and Ionesco, their concern with the possibility of hope, of amelioration, establishes what is clearly a closer affinity with Albee's work. It is particularly ironical, therefore, that Albee should have been accused of writing intensely pessimistic plays at precisely that moment when he was attempting to formulate a tentative but nonetheless hopeful response. In *The Ballad of the Sad Café*, possibly as a reaction to this misunderstanding, he tries to define more directly the terms on which man may confront his situation, while retreating neither into despair nor embittered stoicism.

The world described by Carson McCullers is an unattractive and solitary place. Her characters are grotesque or pathetic (depending on the sensibility of the reader), and find themselves ambiguously balanced between innocence and experience. Indeed the human situation is defined precisely in terms of these bizarre figures: the deaf-mute in *The Heart is a Lonely Hunter*, the hunchbacked dwarf and the giant asexual woman in *The Ballad of the Sad Café*. They obviously have a metaphorical force. Their afflictions are physical proofs of their isolation—an isolation felt most acutely by the adolescent heroine of *The Member of the Wedding* who "belonged to no club and was a member of nothing in the world".[2] Those who are most conscious of this spiritual isolation, retreat into fantasy worlds which ironically serve to alienate them further from their fellow men. Mick, the young heroine of *The Heart is a Lonely Hunter*, is intensely aware of "how lonesome a person could be in a crowded house", but her dreams of becoming a concert pianist require that she find "some good private place where she could go and be by herself".[3] The central situation of the McCullers' hero, then, is that defined by Jake Blount in the same novel when he speaks of himself as being a stranger in a strange land.

Mrs McCullers' concern with the grotesque and the pathetic rarely, however, slips into sentimentality, precisely because she always insists on facing what she takes to be the reality of human isolation. Certainly, under the guise of tolerance for the adolescent and the bemused, she has devoted her talent to tearing away illusions in a way which is distinctly reminiscent of Albee. She has little sympathy, for example, with the young Negro in *Clock without Hands* who confesses: "A lot of my life I've had to make up stories because the real, actual was either too dull or too hard to take"[4]; for it is precisely

[2] Carson McCullers, *The Ballad of the Sad Café: The Novels and Stories of Carson McCullers* (Boston 1951), p. 599.

[3] *Op. cit.*, p. 195.

[4] Carson McCullers, *Clock Without Hands* (Harmondsworth 1965), p. 125.

this which has prevented him from coming to terms with the real world and, more importantly, with other people. So, too, when she advances love as a possible response to the human condition, she does so with the repeated warning that it is no panacea. In fact, if she has one dominant fault, it is that the consistency with which her protagonists are mismated is itself a form of self-indulgence which brings her work at times to the verge of a kind of personal formalism.

Yet, if the world which she describes seems to be a bleak one, it is nonetheless true that all her work is ultimately an "affirmation of the dignity of life",[5] a phrase which she applied to her most recent novel, *Clock without Hands*. For, if her vision reveals man as imperfect and even grotesque, this is an expression of her compassionate sensitivity to the plight of a being who is subject to the irrationality of nature and the distortion of spiritual aspiration. It expresses, too, the closeness of her viewpoint and the extent of her observation, which takes in not only the human form, but also the imperfection which to her, as to Hawthorne, is a mark of humanity. In *Clock without Hands* she uses the image of a man looking down from an aircraft to express her own sense of the self-delusion of those who see the world as a regulated and patterned whole and who are unwilling to face the fact of human isolation:

> the earth assumes order. . . . The earth is finite. From this height you do not see man and the details of his humiliation. The earth from a great distance is perfect and whole. But this is an order foreign to the heart and to love the earth you must come closer.

To love the world, then, as Galsworthy had said, and ultimately to love and understand man, is to accept the need to face his imperfections. For only by so doing, Mrs

[5] Ihab Hassan, *Radical Innocence: Studies in the Contemporary American Novel* (Princeton 1961), p. 227.

McCullers insists, can you hope to come close enough to see beyond appearance and into the soul.

> You see the secret concerns of all the sad back yards. . . .
> From the air men are shrunken and they have an automatic look, like wound-up dolls. They seem to move mechanically among haphazard miseries. You do not see their eyes. And finally this is intolerable. The whole earth from a great distance means less than one long look into a pair of human eyes. Even the eyes of the enemy.[6]

The setting for *The Ballad of the Sad Café* is a lonely town some distance away from the nearest community which is itself significantly called Society City. Immediately, then, we are moving into metaphor. The first character to whom we are introduced by the narrator is the pathetic figure of Miss Amelia, who peers out of her decaying house in the best traditions of Faulkner's Miss Emily. In the novel her description is given with some detail. She is old "with two gray crossed eyes which are turned inward so sharply that they seem to be exchanging with each other one long and secret gaze of grief".[7] This image of human isolation turning in on itself for consolation could be applied to virtually any of Mrs McCullers' protagonists; and clearly here the lonely town and the solitary woman are merely two expressions of the same thing, for Mrs McCullers and Albee alike describe the setting in terms which could apply equally well to its inhabitants, "lonesome—sad—like a place that is far off and estranged from all other places in the world".[8] Both novel and play are concerned with describing the events which have brought Miss Amelia, a muscular and asexual woman, from her position as the town's chief entrepreneur to this current

[6] *Clock Without Hands*, p. 202.
[7] *The Novels and Stories*, p. 3.
[8] *B.S.C.*, p. 3.

isolation. We learn that when young she had been courted by a profligate, called Marvin Macy, whose love for the grotesque woman had reformed him overnight. But after the marriage, Miss Amelia had thrown him out, for, although she had been happy to accept the presents with which he showered her, she was indignant at his attempts to consummate their union. Macy, minus a tooth, leaves town swearing vengeance and promptly reverts to his former life. Later in time, although it is the first major incident of both novel and play, a hunch-backed dwarf, Cousin Lymon, comes into town and claims kinship with Miss Amelia. To the surprise of the whole community she takes him in, and the love which she evidently feels for the dwarf transforms her, as Marvin Macy's love had changed him. She ceases to be a coldly-calculating business woman and opens her store as a café, providing the town with the heart it had formerly lacked. After several years have passed, Marvin Macy returns, and the dwarf is immediately infatuated with him, thus completing a grotesque love triangle. Together they humiliate Amelia, and eventually she and Marvin come to blows. Miss Amelia is on the point of beating her husband when Cousin Lymon leaps on her back and turns the tables. She is beaten senseless, and the two men leave together, having destroyed the café. Amelia, we are told, waits for three years and then has her house boarded up and lives as a recluse. The play ends, as does the book, with the chain gang, whose singing brings the only sound of harmony to an otherwise silent and solitary town.

In one sense the play represents Albee's attempt to rescue the moral of *Who's Afraid of Virginia Woolf?* from those who would see in its ending merely an echo of a Tennessee Williams' sexual resolution. The point of that play had not been that Martha and George were about to march coyly up to their bedroom, like characters out of *A Period of Adjustment*, but rather that they had destroyed the barriers to a real, not necessarily a sexual, contact.

Far from elevating sexual love to the level of therapy, Albee has always been intent on recognising its destructive element. The urge to make meaningful contact is one thing, the need to sublimate this in a sexual assault quite another. Nick and Martha do not make genuine contact in their sexual encounter, any more than had Mommy and Daddy in *The American Dream*. *The Ballad of the Sad Café*, therefore, contrasts the bizarre effects of sexual attraction—emphasised here by the deliberate pairing of the manly and giant Miss Amelia with a homosexual dwarf—with the severely limited but nevertheless real contact symbolised by the members of the chain gang.

In both *The Zoo Story* and *Who's Afraid of Virginia Woolf?* Albee had acknowledged love to be a strange admixture of attraction and revulsion, violence and submission. It clearly plays the same ambiguous role here: an expression perhaps of the tentative nature of Albee's response. When Marvin Macy writes a farewell letter to the wife who has thrown him out, for example, his words underline the paradox: "I hate you. I love you... I loved you for two years 'fore I even dared to speak my love for you, you... you no-good rotten cross-eyed ugly lump!"[9] So that, if love is capable of bringing a dead town and a sterile woman to life, it is equally capable of stimulating a destructive violence. But the "teaching emotion", as Jerry had insisted in the *Zoo Story*, is precisely this mixture of pain and happiness, a blend which, like Miss Amelia's liquor, opens the heart to truth; "A man may suffer or he may be spent with joy—but he has warmed his soul and seen the message hidden there."[10] The power of love is thus great, but also by nature ambiguous and impermanent. So the twelve townspeople who enter the store on the night of its transformation, like the twelve members of the chain gang, are, for a moment, united. If they revert

[9] *B.S.C.*, pp. 101-2.   [10] *B.S.C.*, pp. 14-15.

to their former isolation, they have at least been inducted into that secret of communion which Albert Camus has called "the kind of solidarity which is born in chains".[11]

Albee, then, is insisting on the need to recognise a brotherhood which has nothing to do with social theories or political dogmas, but which grows out of human need. Just as Jerry, in *The Zoo Story*, comes eventually to recognise an urge for genuine contact in the advances of his repulsive landlady and her grotesque dog, so Albee and Mrs McCullers recognise the capacity of these bewildered characters for a contact which emerges from their common situation. Thus, when the Negro maid, Berenice, in *The Member of the Wedding*, says that "no matter what we do we still caught . . . Everybody is caught one way or another",[12] she is not merely voicing that sense of romantic regret that we find in Tennessee Williams. She is, in fact, touching on the very essence of Mrs McCullers' dialectic, for it is precisely this sense of common bondage which to her is both man's curse and the eventual source of his blessing.

The play, we are told by the narrator, is a description of "How we came to . . . silence".[13] This, however, is not wholly accurate, for the play concludes with the "sombre and joyful" music of the prisoners and not with the silence of the enervated town. The distinction is an important one. For, although the townspeople share a similar potential for community, they remain blindly unaware of the chains which link them and which make human contact a necessary and a possible thing. They remain throughout, as Albee had once characterised Broadway audiences, "placid cows". Cousin Lymon, Miss Amelia, and Marvin Macy at least react with passion: not so those around them. Indeed it would not be too fanciful to look on these townsfolk as Albee's

---

[11] Albert Camus, *The Rebel*, tr. Anthony Bowen (London 1953), p. 23.
[12] *The Novels and Stories*, p. 740.   [13] *B.S.C.*, p. 4.

conscious image for an audience who are offered the truth but who remain finally unaffected by the insights presented to them. They observe, accept a vicarious thrill, and then retreat into their former passivity and isolation.

Time magazine saw in *Who's Afraid of Virginia Woolf?* what it took to be a lack of compassion on the part of the author. Mistaking the cruelty of the dialogue for the essence of his dialectic, it failed to distinguish between method and substance. *The Ballad of the Sad Café* might be thought to provoke a similar response, for the use of deformed actors clearly invokes further difficulties, since the action can slip easily into sentimentality or a kind of distasteful exhibitionism. The ambiguous response of the critics makes it clear, however, that Albee has trodden this particular tight-rope with skill. For while Robert Brustein complained that Amelia was presented as being "too cumbrous and lumpish",[14] Henry Hewes found her "a healthy tomboy . . . an eminently lovable girl".[15] This would seem to suggest that Albee has succeeded in avoiding both extremes; surely a mark both of his ability as a dramatist and of the compassion which does in fact lie at the heart of all his work.

His concern here with the grotesque does not grow out of his desire to shock a middle-class audience, nor is it an expression of his resort to the sort of sentimentality which Yeats has defined as unearned emotion. Rather it grows out of an awareness which he shares with the Swiss dramatist, Friedrich Dürrenmatt, who has pointed out that

Our world has led to the grotesque as well as the atom bomb and Hieronymus' madness is with us again; the apocalyptic vision has become the grotesquely real.

[14] Robert Brustein, "The Playwright as Impersonator", *The New Republic*, 16 Nov. 1963, p. 29.
[15] Henry Hewes, "Dismemberment of the Wedding", *Saturday Review*, 16 Nov. 1963, p. 54.

But the grotesque is only a way of expressing in a tangible manner, of making us perceive physically the paradoxical, the form of the unformed, the face of a world without face; and just as in our thinking today we seem to be unable to do without the concept of the paradox, so also in art.[16]

In a world in which men are united only by their common isolation paradox clearly is fundamental; and Albee's concern with the grotesque becomes an important element in the modern vision. At the same time the final scene of the play, as of *The Zoo Story* and *Who's Afraid of Virginia Woolf?*, underlines the potential for human contact which still survives even in a world in which human lives are distorted by unfulfilled desires. The apocalyptic alternative, recognised by Dürrenmatt and identifiable in *Who's Afraid of Virginia Woolf?*, is not apparent here, though, except that in this lonely town "there are no children's voices".[17] Essentially the play is a lament over those who fail to recognise their kinship. The action hangs somewhere between comedy and tragedy; and, as Thomas Mann has remarked, "[modern art] sees life as tragi-comedy, with the result that the grotesque is its most genuine style".[18]

In many ways Albee's suspicion of adaptations is ironically confirmed by his own attempt, for there are certain marked differences between Mrs McCullers' work and his own which do little to advance his reputation. The history of Marvin Macy's relationship with Miss Amelia, which is given little space or emphasis in Mrs Cullers' version, becomes virtually one third of his own. This adds little of significance and seems to derive out of a wish to expand a short novella into a full length play rather than out of anything one might

[16] Toby Cole, *Playwrights on Playwriting* (London 1960), p. 136.
[17] *B.S.C.*, p. 150.
[18] William Van O'Connor, *The Grotesque: An American Genre and Other Essays* (Carbondale 1962), p. 5.

call dramatic necessity. In a play in which a giant woman loves a dwarf who is in turn infatuated by an ex-convict, there is certainly no need for an excessively prolonged demonstration of the dawning of irrational love.

At the same time, Albee is obviously overwhelmed by the problem of turning the novelist's narration into dialogue "which sounds as though it were written by Carson McCullers".[19] Albee has said that there are only two lines of dialogue in the original novella. In fact there are close to a hundred, none of which resort to the rather laboured dialect which he employs. In transposing her simple dialogue into what he clearly takes to be a rural idiom, he is, therefore, in danger of moving the story out of its mythic context into a purely folk one. While he never approaches the phonetic excesses of Eugene O'Neill, his handling of language becomes embarrassingly and uncharacteristically awkward. For the townspeople he devises a clipped and stylised language, while for the poetic and subtly-controlled voice of the author he substitutes a narrator in whose mouth Mrs McCullers' descriptions verge on the merely rhetorical. The remarks of this narrator, moreover, are largely either a substitute for dramatic action or an unnecessary comment on that action. When the long flashback of Marvin Macy's courtship of Miss Amelia ends, the narrator enters to offer the purely gratuitous information that "so ended the ten days of marriage of Miss Amelia Evans and Marvin Macy".[20]

An additional factor which has greatly disturbed several critics is that in the New York production the role of the narrator was played by a Negro actor, for this seems to introduce matters which are largely extraneous to the play's central theme. Obviously, though, he is not entirely irrelevant to a play which, on one level at least,

[19] "Edward Albee Interviewed by Digby Diehl", p. 70.
[20] B.S.C., p. 107.

parodies the idea of Southern womanhood. For Miss Amelia is as much a parody of the Southern gentle-woman as is Faulkner's Temple Drake, while, like the same author's Miss Emily, she ends up a solitary and decaying image of the land which she inhabits, shut up in a building which is itself in a state of decay. She, like the land itself, is unable to come to terms with her own humiliation. If this is a legitimate implication of the play's action and of the implied contrast between the sophistication of the Negro narrator and the primitive reactions of the white townspeople, it is hardly of immediate relevance to Albee's central theme—the nature of human isolation. In Carson McCullers' earlier work the Negro had been the living embodiment of that isolation; while here his presence seems gratuitous and unexplained, and his role both indefinite and unnecessary. There seems to be some justification, in fact, for Richard Kostelanetz's comment that "Albee's decision to retain the narrator is the clumsiest note of all ... his entrances and exits (are) as graceless as rolling a barrel across the stage".[21]

Albee's *The Ballad of the Sad Café*, therefore, while taking his concern with the plight of modern man an important stage further, is at best a disappointing successor to *Who's Afraid of Virginia Woolf?* It seems to prove that in sacrificing his own "voice", his freedom to define character and situation through his command of language, he has sacrificed the essence of his greatness. He has produced a play of disturbing power, a play which Henry Hewes has described as "the most fascinating and evocative piece of work by an American playwright this season",[22] but perhaps this is no great recommendation in a season in which no play was judged to be worthy even of the highly suspect Pulitzer Prize. Certainly it

---

[21] Richard Kostelanetz, "Albee's Sad Café", *Sewanee Review*, LXXII (1964), p. 726.
[22] "Dismemberment of the Wedding", p. 54.

is a play which finally fails either to live up to the promise of his earlier work or to reflect the subtle insight which is the essence of Carson McCullers' particular achievement.

Following *Tiny Alice*, in January 1966, Albee once more attempted an adaptation, this time dramatising a novel by James Purdy, a former Spanish teacher from Lawrence College, who considers himself a "reject" from society and lives "in exile" in Brooklyn. It is hardly surprising that Albee should have been attracted to his work, for both men share a similar view of the continuing decay of their own country. Purdy is what Albee would call a "demonic social critic". At the heart of all his work lies the failure of modern America, its concern with money, success, and marketable sexuality at the cost of a genuine relationship with reality, communal fulfilment, and love. For him the American Dream has become quite literally the American Nightmare, and it is just this nightmare which provides the impetus for his work.

If Purdy's denunciations of American society have been at times more stringent than Albee's, then there cannot, I think, be much doubt that Albee's increasing impatience with a seemingly myopic audience is rapidly bringing him to the point at which he would agree both with the substance and the tone of the following jeremiad contained in a letter by Purdy:

All of my work is a criticism of the United States, implicit not explicit. . . . This is a culture based on money and competition, [it] is inhuman, terrified of love, sexual and other, obsessed with homosexuality and brutality. Our entire moral life is pestiferous and we live in a completely immoral atmosphere. . . . I believe the human being under capitalism is a stilted, depressed, sick creature, that marriage in the United States is homosexuality, and homosexuality a real disease, that we toil and enjoy and live for all the wrong reasons, and that our national life is a nightmare of noise, ugliness, filth and confusion. ... I don't believe America has any future.[23]

If Albee would dissent from any part of that credo, it would be the last seven words, but in *Malcolm*, his adaptation of Purdy's surrealistic novel, it must be doubted if even this exception need be made.

The play, which is undoubtedly Albee's poorest effort to date, is concerned with Malcolm, a boy of fifteen, who is first seen sitting on a bench in front of a large hotel—waiting. When Mr Cox, an astrologer, tries to persuade him to move, he explains that he is waiting for his father. Eventually, however, Cox manages to convince him that he should leave the bench by giving him a series of addresses which, when followed up, bring Malcolm into contact with a number of bizarre characters. His rapid rise to success—a millionaire tries to adopt him, and he marries a "pop-singer"—is a parody of the American Dream. For Malcolm remains as blissfully unaware of the corruption and sterility of the world into which he has moved as had Lemuel Pitkin in Nathanael West's bitter satire, *A Cool Million*. Little by little he becomes tainted by the world; and eventually, having been used and abused, he dies of an excess of alcohol and sexual intercourse and ascends into the heavens on his golden bench.

Malcolm's life is presented as an image of the modern experience. His decision to leave his bench effectively marks his birth, while his passing contacts, established only to be broken again, act as picaresque images of the fragmented existence of contemporary man. As R. W. B. Lewis has pointed out, "in a time characterised so widely by the sense of 'cosmic homelessness', the image of

[23] Webster Schott, "James Purdy: American Dreams", *The Nation*, 23 Mar. 1964, p. 300.

the anxious journey—of life as a succession of provisional
encounters—very naturally suggests itself to the watchful
novelist".[24] Malcolm's encounters constitute his search
for knowledge in a world in which "Innocence has the
appearance of stupidity"[25] and politeness and honesty
are seen as irreconcilables. Cut off from his father and
from the values which he had represented, he looks for a
new guide and finds him in the Mephistophelian figure of
Professor Cox. He it is who introduces Malcolm to
wealth and to sensual indulgence, and who, in doing so,
alienates him completely from his former purity.
Cynical and self-centred, he is a fitting guide to a society
so completely bereft of human values.

The various addresses which Professor Cox presses on
the young boy rapidly introduce him to the hypocrisy of
marriage (Laureen and Kermit Raphaelson), the
corruption of wealth (the Girards) and the prostitution
of art (Jerome and Eloisa Brace). By degrees also he
comes to realise the central importance of money to
this corrupt society. He himself is bought and sold
several times and eventually comes to accept this as
being "as natural as anything in the world".[26] In a
world in which, as Purdy says, "People are occupied
with the world and making money",[27] the fundamentals
of life are ignored, and the mere sight of a cheque is
enough to remove one "from all other human contact".[28]
Malcolm, in other words, is yet another manifestation
of the Young Man in *The American Dream* who had
suffered "a departure of innocence" which had left him
"drained, torn asunder" and unable to "feel love".

Once again, it is important, however, to make a
distinction between Beckett's maimed characters, whose
disabilities signify a fundamentally aberrant world, and

[24] *The Picaresque Saint*, p. 150.
[25] *M.*, p. 9.   [26] *M.*, p. 86.
[27] James Purdy, *Children is All* (New York 1962), p. 172.
[28] James Purdy, *Malcolm* (London 1960), p. 147.

Albee's grotesque parodies of American absurdity. Clearly in a society in which, as Purdy suggests, "people are losing their character as real people",[29] the grotesque is once again a natural idiom, but equally clearly there is a ready acceptance of the existence of "real people". The surreal world presented in *Malcolm*, therefore, is not a comment on the essence of the human condition, but a grotesque image of a spiritually and morally deformed society—a society, moreover, which is identifiable as American.

In the New York production, as Robert Brustein informs us, Professor Cox was rather pointedly dressed as Uncle Sam, while Kermit, who is either 192 (War of Independence) or 97 (Civil War), wore the uniform of a Confederate soldier. Similarly, when Malcolm is taken to a prostitute as part of his "education", she significantly gives him a memento of his visit which incorporates the American flag. The corruption, then, is an American one, a point which Purdy emphasises in his subsequent novel, *The Nephew*. Here, when the American flag is taken out for the annual Independence Day celebrations, it is rotting, an obvious symbol of a society which is itself in a decayed condition. As Purdy says of the woman who holds the flag, "She was certain she could mend Old Glory. . . . But the tear was not so easily repaired. . . . Other long-hidden snags and rents in the material asserted themselves . . . and soon Alma saw that what she held in her hand was a tissue of rotten cloth, impossible to mend."[30]

In apparently suggesting that the failure of American society is absolute and irreparable, Purdy seems to be close to embracing a rather despairing fatalism. Certainly Professor Cox implies just such a determinism when he

[29] Warren French, "The Quaking World of James Purdy", in *Essays in Modern American Literature*, ed. Richard E. Longford (Stetson U.P. 1963), p. 113.

[30] James Purdy, *The Nephew* (London 1961), p. 195.

demands that the characters "act out the parts they are meant to act out with one another",[31] and adds that "There's just no help for it—Everything is played out".[32] But this is a stance which Albee has consistently criticised, and which Purdy himself has disavowed. For, while insisting that "We live in the stupidest cultural era of American history", he has likewise insisted that he does not see despair in his writing.[33] He does in fact offer an implicit antidote to the desperate situation which he describes. For the anti-heroic figure of Malcolm clearly bears an antithetical relation to Purdy's central message. He refuses to recognise his own freedom to act. Like Saul Bellow's Augie March, he accedes to the wills and values of those around him. But where Bellow's protagonist finally rebels against this process, and realises that, "I didn't want to be ... determined ... and wouldn't become what other people wanted to make me",[34] Malcolm remains blissfully unaware of his manipulation. Professor Cox launches him on his "education" as though the only alternative to his original isolation is to join in the frenzied pursuit of money, success, and sexual dominance. The implicit theme of both novel and play, therefore, as of *Who's Afraid of Virginia Woolf?*, is the need for the individual to abandon a spurious existence in favour of a real world in which human values can reassert themselves. Thus Purdy has said, "I suppose one of the themes of my work is that you must accept yourselves and others, whatever they are ...".[35] For, as Bellow makes Augie March remark, "When striving stops, the truth comes as a gift—bounty, harmony, love, and so forth".[36] Albee makes this point more explicitly, for he grants to Mme Girard a percep-

[31] *Malcolm*, p. 98.
[32] *Ibid.*
[33] "James Purdy: American Dreams", p. 302.
[34] Saul Bellow, *The Adventures of Augie March* (London 1954), p. 117.
[35] "James Purdy: American Dreams", p. 302.
[36] *The Adventures of Augie March*, p. 514.

tion which Purdy does not allow her in the novel. She
alone understands that the central failure of her society
is its lack of compassion—a perception which earns her
the right to join Malcolm in his ascension.

The sheer enormity of American callousness and the
extent of its corruption, as seen by Albee, is emphasised,
as this reference to ascension would suggest, by a sub-
structure of Christian symbolism. For not only does this
society destroy and corrupt the innocent, it even
corrupts God himself.

At the beginning of the play Malcolm sits on his
bench and is as isolated from real human contact as
Peter had been in *The Zoo Story*. He sees no purpose in
leaving his refuge and spends his time waiting for his
father, as Beckett's characters had awaited the arrival
of Godot. Although it would be as dangerous to look
for a precise allegory in *Malcolm* as it is to look for it in
Waiting for Godot, it would be peevish to deny the Christian overtones of the play. For Malcolm, Purdy pointedly
informs us, was born in December and thus entered a
world in which "he had perhaps never belonged".[37]
At first he is totally ignorant of this world into which he
has been cast and remembers only what is clearly an
adamic existence in which "My father seemed to feel I was
always going to stay just the way I was . . . We were both
satisfied . . . We were very happy together, my father and
I."[38] Now, however, he is clearly in a fallen world, and
all that he can remember of the precepts of a former age
are fragments of the simple pieties, "I will try to be all
that you have taught me . . . polite; honest; and . . .
what's the rest of it, father?"[39] Malcolm, then, is clearly
a potential saviour; and, when Madame Girard, the
wife of the millionaire, shouts out in awe, "Royalty . . . A
prince has come among us!",[40] it is obvious that society is
witnessing a Second Coming. Its response to this event

[37] *Malcolm*, p. 216.   [38] *M.*, p. 8.
[39] *M.*, p. 12.   [40] *M.*, p. 36.

is not, however, a sudden resurgence of love in the face of such innocence, but rather a desire to corrupt and own this phenomenon. In this it is entirely successful, for it gradually succeeds in converting him to its own cynical disillusionment. At the beginning of the play he insists that his father has merely disappeared and urgently questions all those he meets as to his whereabouts. Madame Girard typifies her society when she callously remarks that: "I . . . do not think your father exists . . . I have *never* thought he did. . . . And what is more . . . *nobody* thinks he exists . . . or ever *did* exist."[41] Malcolm's shocked reply, "That's blasphemy", obviously reinforces the play's Christian overtones, but by the end of the play he himself comes to accept the popular opinion that his father is dead. Evidently his rise to success and his corresponding movement towards corruption have reached some sort of climax, so that now, when he finally sees a man whom he takes to be his father, the man denies any such connexion, and Malcolm's cry of "Father! Father!" goes unanswered. He is ready now for the crucifixion which has become almost the conventional ending to an Albee play, and indeed the young boy dies shortly afterwards, killed by those Faustian excesses which Albee had attacked in *Who's Afraid of Virginia Woolf?* He returns, presumably, to his former existence, having made a sacrifice for which Professor Cox had in part prepared us earlier in the play when he had stressed that "It is the fate of sages and saints, I suppose, to serve, teach . . . *give*, if you will, of their substance . . . and be abandoned in the end".[42] It is the sad irony of Albee's play that Malcolm makes his sacrifice without having taught or even himself understood his gospel in a world entirely alien to the kind of contact and love which he clearly craves and values. He ascends into the heavens having failed to redeem a people who can corrupt even the primally innocent. In the novel we are left with an

[41] *M.*, p. 33.   [42] *M.*, p. 51.

empty tomb, in the play with an ascension, but in both the dismal failure of this divine intervention is made clear.

All that remains of Malcolm is Eloisa Brace's portrait, a relic of the innocence which they have destroyed and of the love which they have ignored. Innocence can apparently be admired only so long as it is not a real and immediate alternative. But neither Albee nor Purdy are sentimentalists simply regretting a loss of innocence, for Malcolm demonstrates all too clearly that innocence is as close to naïveté and even stupidity as it is to purity. Purdy's constant use of children as protagonists, therefore, is not merely a device for balancing the innocence of the child against the corruption of society. It is also a direct expression of his own conviction that "There don't seem to be any men and women in America; there are those who are young and have everything before them—and then there are the others, mostly dead".[43] There are those, that is, who have faith in the Dream and those who have discovered, too late, its nightmare quality. So it is that Kermit and Laureen Raphaelson, like George and Martha before them, are referred to as "Grown up children". For their touching faith in the significance of the social charade is final proof of their immaturity. More seriously, they remain entirely oblivious of the self-annihilating nature of a society which denies the compassion necessary for its own survival. In this sense Purdy's and Albee's vision is a good deal bleaker than, say, Melville's, for in *Billy Budd* innocence is simply put to death. In *Malcolm*, more ominously, it is seduced and enrolled in the ranks of society before being discarded like a broken component. Decay is now more firmly rooted, and there is thus a bitter irony at the end of the play when the characters join together and mildly regret that "he didn't have the stuff",[44] blissfully unaware that after the Second Coming there lies only the apocalypse.

[43] "James Purdy: American Dreams", p. 302.   [44] *M.*, p. 138.

Nor is the apocalypse to be long delayed. For in the play Malcolm is acutely aware that "THE WHOLE WORLD IS FLYING APART!!",[45] while in the novel the same perception is implicit in an ominous sense of decay. Purdy explains that "one felt that it was afternoon, late afternoon breaking into twilight . . . like perpetual autumn, an autumn that will not pass into winter owing to some damage perhaps to the machinery of the cosmos . . . slowly everything will begin to fall piece by piece, the walls will slip down . . .".[46] On the very verge of this cataclysm, the characters still continue their ceaseless campaigns of sensual indulgence and material satisfaction blind to the gulf which is opening up under their feet.

Purdy, like William Burroughs, is characteristically concerned with this moment of final disintegration: his one-act play, Cracks, being actually set at the moment of the apocalypse. In the face of this imminent dissolution, he, like Albee, can accept elements of the Christian message, but not Christ himself. He insists on the urgency of human love rather than divine intervention. For the God which presides over this decay is for the most part a pathetic figure. In Cracks he is simply a rank incompetent while in another story, "Sermon", he is a ranting maniac. Like the "old pot" whom Malcolm recognises as his "father", this deity has no real control over his own creation. For the Hell which Purdy describes, like that detailed so exhaustively by Henry Miller in The Air-Conditioned Nightmare, is essentially of man's own making. It is a Hell which, like Dostoyevsky's, derives its essence from the total absence of love. Beneath the sexual cupidity and the frantic materialism, there is no real human contact and no urge towards establishing any. To both Purdy and Albee, then, the country that was to have been a new Eden has become instead a place

[45] M., p. 86.
[46] Malcolm, p. 122.

where greed and inhumanity have finally trampled on the Puritan virtues. As in *The American Dream* and *The Zoo Story*, the individual has surrendered his identity while a generation of nerveless men have abdicated their manhood. So we are back again with Eliot's "hollow men", who slip into oblivion by default, but the hope of the former plays now rests on nothing more solid than Madame Girard's tardy recognition of the need "to love". In *Malcolm* Albee comes closer to despair than in any of his former works.

In adapting the novel for the stage, Albee retained much of the original dialogue but necessarily reduced the number of scenes. He also made certain more significant changes. Kermit, who had been a midget in the novel, now becomes a two hundred year old man, possibly to avoid a visual rhyme with *The Ballad of the Sad Café*, but more probably to establish his symbolic force as an archetypal American. It is worthwhile noting here that George jokingly assigns the same age to Martha in *Who's Afraid of Virginia Woolf?* Perhaps the most important change which he makes, though, is that he assigns multiple roles to certain actors. The actor who plays the part of Professor Cox also plays a brothel-keeper, a wash-room attendant, and a doctor, while the actress who plays Laureen Raphaelson also plays a streetwalker and the madame of a local brothel. Cox thus becomes kin to such creations as Melville's Confidence Man and Ralph Ellison's Rineheart (in *Invisible Man*), both of whom benefit from the corruption of the society in which they operate. As Ellison has said of Rineheart, he is "the personification of chaos. He is also intended to represent America and change. He has lived so long with chaos that he knows how to manipulate it."[47] This is true also of Cox, who, made up to look like Uncle Sam, presides over a disintegrating society, his changing roles demonstrating his own corruption and his ability to

[47] Ralph Ellison, *Shadow and Act* (London 1967), p. 181.

diagnose and encourage corruption in others. His very name signifies his command of events.

But not all the changes can be granted this conscious logic. For, if there are genuine doubts as to the seriousness of the work which Albee has produced since *Who's Afraid of Virginia Woolf?*, these must crystallise around *Malcolm*, which is at times a pretentious and even a careless piece of work. In a very real sense, Purdy's novel has a greater internal logic than has Albee's play, for in adapting it for the stage he has been all too ready to sacrifice coherence to convenience, until, at times, the surreal is in danger of becoming the frankly mystifying. Thus when Malcolm is offered his first address by Professor Cox, he is horrified and throws the visiting card away. In the novel there is some logic in this action, since the boy is disgusted to find that the address is that of an undertaker. Albee, however, while omitting the figure of the undertaker entirely, curiously retains the boy's reaction, merely transferring it to Kermit and Laureen Raphaelson. His disgusted reaction now makes no apparent sense. Indeed in the novel the boy had responded favourably to this further address, even commenting on the beauty of the names. Similarly, in the course of his encounter with the undertaker, in Purdy's version, Malcolm is told to go away and return in twenty years. His dismayed shout, "It's Not twenty years",[48] shortly before his death thus makes some kind of sense. Albee, however, chooses to retain this despairing cry, while omitting the original incident which gives it its meaning. Thus Purdy's oblique approach becomes even more opaque when transferred to the stage.

As in *The Ballad of the Sad Café*, Albee continues to show a marked tendency to substitute self-conscious rhetoric for revealed action. Girard Girard's unctuous comment, that "Between simile and metaphor lies all

[48] *M.*, p. 221.

the sadness in the world",[49] is a precious exhibition of Albee's own mastery of the aphorism rather than proof of the character's poetic sensibility. In fact Albee is never far away from self-parody. For the genuine insight of his earlier plays he now substitutes a pseudo-profundity, suggesting a deeper significance than the play can support Thus when Laureen Raphaelson offers Malcolm the information that "We have fifteen cats",[50] Albee makes her add the sententiously baffling question, "Am I getting across to you?"—a remark calculated to bewilder any audience, while sending the literary critic scrambling for his reference books.

Malcolm was for the most part poorly received by critics and public alike and was taken off five days after its opening. In general it was greeted with blank incomprehension, while theatre critics united in dismissing it as obscure and pretentious. To Robert Brustein it was merely "one of those squashy allegories of lost innocence first introduced into the theatre by Tennessee Williams". He saw it, moreover, as evidence of what he takes to be Albee's tendency "to get more abstract and incoherent until he is finally reduced, as here, to nervous plucking at broken strings".[51] To Robert Corrigan the play was an example of "Pop Theatre", a "kind of medieval Fellini through Tom Wolfe . . . which in the end didn't mean very much".[52] Certainly it seems clear that Purdy's surrealistic images do not translate well into dramatic form, and one suspects that what Mme Girard says to Malcolm at one stage in the novel might well be applied to Albee's play, "Texture is all . . . substance nothing".[53] For one finally gets the impression that Albee is attempting to bully his audience by sheer strength of will into sharing his perceptions and into

[49] *M.*, p. 48.   [50] *M.*, p. 16.
[51] Robert Brustein, "Albee's Allegory of Innocence", *The New Republic*, 29 Jan. 1966, p. 36.
[52] Robert W. Corrigan, "Malcolm Didn't Mean Very Much", *Vogue*, 15 Feb. 1966, p. 56.   [53] *M.*, p. 91.

accepting his surreal approach. He is in danger of demanding too much, of failing to establish a direct connexion between the essential experience of the audience and what appears to be a largely alien world. As T. S. Eliot has said, "the explorer beyond the frontiers of ordinary consciousness will only be able to return and report to his fellow-citizens, if he has all the time a firm grasp upon the realities with which they are already acquainted".[54] It is this firm grasp which is seemingly lacking; and, as Brustein has pointed out, there is a real danger that Albee may retreat further and further into a private world where his conversation will be only with himself. This is a danger which clearly exists for Purdy as well, for he is obviously approaching therapy when he says, "I am not even writing novels . . . I am writing *me*. I go on writing to tell myself at least what I have been through."[55] Autism is only one step away.

[54] T. S. Eliot, *Selected Prose* (Harmondsworth 1963), p. 96.
[55] "James Purdy: American Dreams", p. 301.

CHAPTER VI

THE STRATEGY OF MADNESS:
A DELICATE BALANCE

Pirandello used to refer to his own work as the *teatro dello specchio*, the theatre of the looking-glass, because it was concerned with bringing man face to face with the image of his own life. For, as he pointed out:

> When a man lives he lives and does not see himself. Well, put a mirror before him and make him see himself in the act of living. Either he is astonished at his own appearance, or else he turns away his eyes so as not to see himself, or else in disgust he spits at his image, or, again, clenches his fist to break it. In a word, there arises a crisis, and that crisis is my theatre.[1]

This crisis is also the essence of Albee's theatre which from *The Zoo Story* to *A Delicate Balance* concentrates on precisely this moment in which man is made to see himself "in the act of living". His work too is a theatre of the looking-glass devoted to reflecting what to him is a true image of modern man—solitary, impotent, and in retreat from a world which appears to offer nothing but futility. But where Pirandello is content with articulating the dilemma of the individual in a world in which "reality is a mere transitory and fleeting illusion",[2] Albee is concerned with locating the source of a limited but genuine hope. In forcing his protagonist to abandon his protective illusions, he forces him, as he had Peter in *The Zoo Story* and George in *Who's Afraid of Virginia*

---

[1] Quoted in Robert Brustein, *The Theatre of Revolt* (London 1965), p. 290. [2] *Op. cit.*, p. 314.

Woolf?, to the point of commitment. This process lies at the heart of *A Delicate Balance* (1966), which won Albee the Pulitzer Prize denied to his earlier and essentially more worthy play.

Who's Afraid of Virginia Woolf? had examined the impotence of contemporary society; *A Delicate Balance* attempts to penetrate to the fear of which this impotence is merely one expression. Rather like T. S. Eliot's *The Family Reunion*, it tries to delve below the surface of a precarious urbanity to the spiritual terror which exists beneath. In Eliot's words, it is concerned with

> The backward look behind the assurance . . .
>   the backward half-look
> Over the shoulder, towards the primitive terror.[3]

The play is set in the living room of a large and well-appointed suburban house, and the action centres on six characters linked either by familial ties or by the familiarity of long association, which they falsely confuse with "love". Against this setting they act out a ritual which, like those in Eliot's play and Albee's own earlier work, forces them to face the spectres of their own fears.

Agnes and Tobias are approaching sixty, and it is clear that they have evolved a workable relationship which, while protecting them from obvious loneliness, has left them fundamentally estranged from one another. They live with Agnes's sister, an alcoholic who had once been Tobias's mistress. Into this tense but apparently reassuring situation, there intrude their daughter, Julia, returned from the latest of her marital failures, and their "best-friends", Harry and Edna. These three arrivals come in search of comfort, hoping to find some refuge from sudden crises in their own lives. But in this atmosphere, the delicate balance of middle-class temporising is disturbed, and for a moment they are forced into the sort of introspection which can lead either to a deeper

[3] T. S. Eliot, *Four Quartets* (London 1944), p. 29.

perception or back into the anaesthesia of contemporary life. Seeking comfort, they find themselves face to face with their secret fears.

When Harry and Edna arrive, they are terrified, having just undergone a frightening experience which they are unable or unwilling to specify beyond the fact that "it was all very quiet, and we were all alone . . . and then . . . nothing happened, but . . . WE GOT . . . FRIGHTENED . . . We . . . were . . . terrified . . . It was like being lost: very young again, with the dark, and lost."[4] Faced with what William James has called "an irremediable sense of precariousness",[5] and Tolstoy an awareness of the "meaningless absurdity of life",[6] they try to win their way back to "sanity" through contact with the "normal" world of suburban living. But for a moment their eyes have been opened. It is precisely with this moment of enlightenment that Albee is concerned in *A Delicate Balance*. For his characters, like Eliot's,

> are all people
> To whom nothing has happened, at most
>   a continual impact
> Of external events

they

> have gone through life in sleep
> Never woken to the nightmare.[7]

Now they are forced, for a while, to do precisely this: to wake to the nightmare and face their true image in the mirror.

The delicate balance which Agnes and Tobias have contrived in order to survive is not threatened by Claire, who, having been categorised as an alcoholic, can be

[4] *D.B.*, p. 45.

[5] William James, *The Varieties of Religious Experience* (New York 1902), p. 136.

[6] *Op. cit.*, p. 155.

[7] *Collected Plays*, p. 65.

safely ignored. The real threat is implicit in the very strategy by which they live. For accepting, as they do, that the ordered structure of daily routine in turn suggests a kind of "cosmic purpose", any disruption of that routine must imply a disruption of the very foundation of their existence. Sanity can be preserved, therefore, only so long as the artificial order constructed by society remains unthreatened. As Claire points out, "the drunks stay drunk; the Catholics go to Mass, the bounders bound. We can't have changes—throws the balance off. . . . Just think, Tobias, what would happen if the patterns changed; you wouldn't know where you stood, and the world would be full of strangers."[8] Perhaps it is no longer surprising to find that this is an insight shared by Eliot's characters who

> only ask to be reassured
> About the noises in the cellar
> And the window that should not have been open

and who desperately advise themselves to "Hold tight, hold tight, we must insist that the world is what we have always taken it to be".[9]

When the precarious balance of this compromise is threatened, there remains only the retreat into illusion. In Claire's case this involves a simple resort to alcohol, but Albee is concerned here with a final and more dangerous subterfuge—complete alienation from a threatening reality. When the play opens Agnes is considering the possiblity of going mad, becoming a schizophrenic, "since I speculate I might, some day, or early evening I think more likely—some autumn dusk— go quite mad, then I very well might".[10] As the action of the play takes place on just such an autumn evening, there can be little doubt that the "insanity" does ensue and

[8] *D.B.*, p. 144.
[9] *Collected Plays*, p. 74.
[10] *D.B.*, p. 4.

that, far from offering a protection, it precipitates a sudden and frightening awareness of absurdity. Moreover, it seems likely that Edna and Harry, who are described by Albee as being "Very much like Agnes and Tobias", are to be taken as representing the other half of the schizophrenic personality, for in a real sense they act as substitutes for those whose home they have effectively taken over; Edna herself taking on the role and function of the mother, while Harry is actually referred to as "being Tobias".[11] Thus, while the friends can be granted a separate identity, they can also be seen as expressions of the suppressed fears of Agnes and Tobias.

R. D. Laing has pointed out that "the behaviour that gets labelled schizophrenic is a special strategy that a person invents in order to live in an unlivable situation".[12] To Agnes it is indeed just such a strategy to be employed, "if all else should fail; if sanity, such as it is, should become too much".[13] But as Albee has insisted in *Who's Afraid of Virginia Woolf?*, those who retreat into insanity remain "undeveloped" and incapable of establishing genuine relationships. The danger in real terms, then, is that the protective schizophrenia may become a total substitute for reality—a danger which Agnes recognises when she accepts the chance that "I could not . . . come back".[14] At the very least, Albee insists, such a response must leave the individual totally alone, "a stranger in . . . the world, quite . . . uninvolved".[15]

Clearly what he is calling for here, as in his earlier plays, is a courageous determination to face the world as it is. This indeed is the crux of what Albee sees as the modern dilemma. For he pictures the individual poised on the brink of commitment but finally unwilling to embrace values which differ so radically from those of

---

[11] *D.B.*, p. 103.

[12] R. D. Laing, *The Politics of Experience and the Birds of Paradise* (Harmondsworth 1966), p. 95.

[13] *D.B.*, p. 10.   [14] *Ibid.*   [15] *D.B.*, p. 3.

society itself. Rather than face the anguish of freedom and responsibility, the individual lapses, like George in *Who's Afraid of Virginia Woolf?* and Claire and Tobias here, into impotence and illusion, sacrificing compassion and human concern to an expedient detachment.

Hence, *A Delicate Balance* is ultimately Albee's acknowledgment of the fact that, "We're not a communal nation"[16] and that there is a desperate need to re-establish human relationships on a firm foundation of truth. For to him, so long as we "submerge our truths" on "the grassy bottom" and prefer to "have our sunsets on untroubled waters", then we are doomed to absurdity. The vital need is to dive down to that submerged truth, to "develop gills".[17] The urgency of this metamorphosis is underlined by Agnes's warning that "Everything becomes . . . too late, finally".[18] As in *Who's Afraid of Virginia Woolf?*, the alternative to the pursuit of truth is apocalypse—a fact which is made clear by Agnes's prophecy of a world ending with nothing more than "rust; bones; and the wind".[19]

To Albee the individual poised between the "leap of faith" which had tempted Julian in *Tiny Alice* and the bourgeois contentment seized upon by Agnes and Tobias, should turn to the one source of possible renewal—man. But it is precisely the failure of the play's characters to do this, to establish the importance of human contact, of love, which is the essence of their predicament. Within this society, as Albee had stressed in *The American Dream*, even the word "love" has become corrupted, being simply a synonym for self-pity and greed, while marriage itself is merely a device for evading the harshness of the real world.

Erich Fromm has suggested that for many marriage is an attempt to counter a feeling of isolation. He argues that for such people, "the main emphasis" is "on finding a

16 *D.B.*, p. 92.   17 *D.B.*, p. 93.
18 *D.B.*, p. 164.   19 *Ibid.*

refuge from an otherwise unbearable sense of aloneness".[20] When this fails, as it does time and again for Julia, such people, "continue to remain children, to hope for father or mother to come to their help when help is needed".[21] This explains why Julia returns to her home and demands access to her own room—a room which, like that in *Who's Afraid of Virginia Woolf?*, clearly functions as a refuge, a womb, "Warmth. A special room with a night light, or the door ajar so that you can look down the hall from the bed and see Mommy's door is open . . . back from the world? To the sadness and reassurance of your parents. . . . You're laying claim to the cave."[22] Julia's insanity— she becomes hysterical and eventually catatonic—is, thus, like her mother's, an expression both of her failure to understand the real nature of love and of her inability to face a world in which the connexion between individuals is continually threatened. As Fromm has pointed out, "If the nature of sanity is to grow out of the womb into the world, the nature of severe mental disease is to be attracted by the womb, to be sucked back into it—and that is to be taken away from life".[23]

Like Julia, Claire, and Agnes, Tobias also has withdrawn from what he sees as the harsher realities of life. He has given up trying to make contact primarily because he is afraid that to love is to become vulnerable. Unable to adjust himself to the loss of his son, Teddy, who had died at the age of two, he refuses to accept the implications of love, choosing rather to substitute a kind of painless coexistence. Such a reaction leads directly to that retreat into privatism which Agnes identifies as "the demise of intensity, the private preoccupations, the substitutions."[24]

If Tobias's distrust of the commitment involved in love is the cause of this isolation, it is also the source both

[20] Eric Fromm, *The Art of Loving* (London 1957), p. 88.
[21] *Op. cit.*, p. 104.   [22] *D.B.*, p. 92.
[23] *The Art of Loving*, pp. 96-7.   [24] *D.B.*, p. 82.

of his guilt and his fear. Indeed, in order to clarify his feelings, he recounts a long parable of his relationship with a cat which in some ways parallels the story of Jerry and the dog in *The Zoo Story*. Tobias's cat, which had lived with him contentedly for fifteen years, had suddenly withdrawn its affection, refusing to stay in the same room, refusing even to purr. Tobias now describes how he had become progressively determined to restore their relationship. His failure in this had quickly turned his affection to hatred, for he had come to feel that the cat's attitude implied an accusation. He felt that he had been betrayed. Finally, when all his advances had been repulsed, he had killed the cat, so that it could no longer reproach him. But now he realises that it is precisely his failure to persevere in love merely because it is not returned which is the source of his sense of guilt. For wrapped up in his own self-concern he had been unable to recognise the urgent need for love and compassion in a world unspeakably bleak without them. In terms of his parable he finally recognises that, "I might have tried longer. I might have gone on, as long as cats live, the same way. I might have worn a hair shirt, locked myself in the house with her, done penance."[25]

This is precisely the response which he finally brings himself to offer to the neighbours who have forced him to the point of involvement. For in the course of the play he gradually feels his way towards an understanding both of the fact of his own isolation and of the real nature of his relationship with those he had taken to be his best friends. He finally admits that he does not love them and confesses that they are a threat to his peace of mind. But by a supreme effort of will he applies the lesson of his own parable. He fights to overcome his own self-interest and in doing so goes some way towards expiating his sense of guilt: "I DON'T WANT YOU HERE! I DON'T LOVE YOU: BUT BY GOD ... YOU STAY!"[26] To Agnes, Edna and

[25] *D.B.*, p. 37.   [26] *D.B.*, p. 162.

Harry represent only the fear which can upset her compromise with existence. She refers to them as a plague, a "mortal illness" which has descended on them, and which must be rejected. To Tobias, however, these two, and thus the terror, the sense of absurdity which they represent, must be embraced and not denied. In so far as he succeeds in doing this, Tobias emerges as one of Albee's "reality-heroes"; a saint who accepts the Old Testament directive to "love the stranger", and who fulfils William James's primary Christian injunction, "a man must die to an unreal life before he can be born to a real life".[27]

By the end of the play, then, Tobias has regained something of his courage and has achieved an insight into his private fears which, logically enough, comes to him as it does to Eliot's protagonist:

> Not in the day time
> And in the hither world
> Where we know what we are doing
> There is not its operation . . .
> But in the night time
> In the nether world.[28]

For to Albee as to Camus, "There is no sun without shadow and it is essential to know the night".[29] So it is significant that of the play's three acts two take place during the night, a time when, as Agnes admits, "we . . . let the demons out" and discover "the dark side of our reason".[30]

Hence it follows that the apparently trite ending should not be taken at face value, for Agnes's expansive welcome of the returning day is clearly Albee's ironical comment on the ease with which the individual rejects

[27] *The Varieties of Religious Experience*, p. 165.
[28] *The Collected Plays*, pp. 121-2.
[29] *The Myth of Sisyphus*, p. 99.
[30] *D.B.*, p. 170.

new insight. Indeed, when Robert Brustein accuses Albee of closing his play "with one of those vibrato rising sun lines familiar from at least a dozen such evenings",[31] he is in danger of misunderstanding the whole point of the play. For to a mind which grasps desperately at the apparent order of daily routine as a welcome escape from the more painful realities of life, the return of day provides an excuse to escape the perceptions of the night. Viewed thus the play's final lines have a pointed irony. Agnes rejects the knowledge which the night has brought and consoles herself with the thought that "when the daylight comes again . . . comes order with it". With Edna and Harry gone, she feels that "we'll all forget . . . quite soon".[32] Tobias, on the other hand, regrets that, "when the daylight comes the pressures will be on, and all the insight won't be worth a damn".[33]

To Albee, Agnes's willing retreat from the brink is finally less significant than Tobias's stumbling perception. Like William James, he believes that "Truly the light is sweet, and a pleasant thing it is for the eyes to behold the sun: but if a man live many years and rejoice in them all yet let him remember the days of darkness . . .".[34] If Tobias's affirmation is only a tentative, even a slightly prevaricating one, perhaps it is an indication of the truth of his earlier insight—an understanding shared by George in *Who's Afraid of Virginia Woolf?*, that, ". . . once you drop you can come back up part way . . . but never really back again"[35]—a clear warning for a society in decline.

The fact still remains that man is free to act. If he chooses again and again to retreat into illusion, and to elevate his own sense of guilt above the need for compassion, it is clear that there is no inevitability in this choice. Here

[31] Robert Brustein, "Albee Decorates an Old House", *The New Republic*, 8 Oct. 1966, p. 36.
[32] *D.B.*, p. 170.   [33] *D.B.*, p. 128.
[34] *The Varieties of Religious Experience*, p. 139.
[35] *D.B.*, p. 24.

is the explanation of Claire's insistence that she is not an alcoholic, although it "would be simpler if I were".[36] Indeed the distinction which she makes between herself and the alcoholics is basically the same distinction which Albee has always been at pains to make between Beckett's passive victims and his own protagonists: "they couldn't help it; I could, and wouldn't . . . they were sick, and I was merely wilful."[37] Agnes, in fact, admits that man's absurdity is largely of his own making: "We manufacture such a proportion of our own despair."[38] The door is thus clearly open for amelioration; and the suffering, which perhaps significantly takes place between Friday and Sunday, can result in redemption.

If Albee is getting more urgent, even, perhaps, more shrill, in his effort to force the need for love in a world seemingly intent on self-destruction and content to find purpose in the sham order of bourgeois society, it is because he is strongly aware of the attractiveness of illusion. Albee is not primarily a social reformer. He is concerned with moral and spiritual reform, but to this he brings all the urgency of the committed. The very fact that he allows the last word to Agnes is, in itself, a demonstration of his growing fear that his is a voice echoing in the wilderness. Indeed it is possible to see *A Delicate Balance* as, in part, an expression of Albee's own sense of artistic frustration: the frustration of a dramatist able to command the attention of an audience in the theatre, but unable to wring from it an admission of the connexion which exists between the enacted drama and their own lives. The audience, like Tobias, "can sit and watch . . . can have . . . so clear a picture, see everybody moving through his own jungle . . . an insight into all the reasons, all the needs . . . the dark sadness".[39] But the return to routine, to daylight, after the performance, means, as we have seen, that, "the insight won't be

[36] *D.B.*, p. 26. [37] *Ibid.*
[38] *D.B.*, p. 126. [39] *D.B.*, p. 128.

worth a damn". So, too, when Agnes speaks of being, "burdened with the ability to view a situation objectively while I'm in it",[40] when she apologises for "being articulate"[41] and adds "if I shout, it's merely to be heard . . . above the awful din of your privacies and sulks",[42] this, too, can ultimately be seen as an expression of Albee's own sense of artistic martyrdom.

Critical response to *A Delicate Balance* was largely hostile. Robert Brustein, writing in *The New Republic*, found the play to be little more than, "an old house which an interior decorator has tried to furnish with reproductions and pieces bought at auction"[43]; while a caustic article in *Newsweek* attacked what it saw as the "inflated dialogue" the "kind of cliché that is all too prominent in Albee's rhetoric".[44] Certainly Albee's idiom lacks the control which it had shown in *Who's Afraid of Virginia Woolf?* More important, however, is the fact that his preoccupation with the metaphysical roles which he ascribes to his characters is in danger of eliminating the very humanity demanded by the terms of his argument. As James Baldwin has said of Camus, one cannot help feeling at times that ideas mean more to him than people.

Albee is always at his weakest with minor characters. They seem to drift through the plays, appearing to act only as butts for humour or as conscious symbols. In this play Claire, whose name emphasises the clarity of her insight, seems to be little more than the stereotype wise drunk. Rather like that inevitable figure in the early films who wanders in and out of the action and manages to survive reasonably intact while fist-fights and custard pies proliferate, she moves uncertainly through the play making wise remarks which can have little validity because she lacks credibility as a character. The same is

[40] *D.B.*, p. 81.   [41] *D.B.*, p. 45.   [42] *D.B.*, p. 80.
[43] "Albee Decorates an Old House", p. 36.
[44] Anon., "Skin Deep," *Newsweek*, 3 Oct. 1966, p. 98.

essentially true of Julia, Harry and Edna. Their symbolic functions take complete control, and they give the impression of being manipulated puppets. Nevertheless, even though his characters forfeit their humanity through their persistent resort to illusion and their acceptance of defined social roles, one is never convinced that their hollowness is merely an expression of this. Rather it is a direct result of Albee's failure to give his characters life. Here then is the central dilemma which he fails to resolve: how to create characters capable of arousing the sympathy of an audience when the demands of his own drama require their reduction to the position of social cyphers.

To an audience becoming increasingly alienated from Albee's experiments, *A Delicate Balance* appeared to be a move towards the naturalistic style familiar on Broadway. To several critics, however, the play's chief fault lay in its mixture of styles. For one, the play moved from "realism to fantasy", to another, perhaps more surprisingly, from "symbolism" to "naturalism". In fact, one of the most important lessons which Albee has to offer to the American theatre is that distinctions such as these no longer make any sense. *A Delicate Balance*, like *Who's Afraid of Virginia Woolf?*, defies such classification. Perhaps the most that can be said is that it represents an attempt to achieve in prose what Eliot had sought to achieve in verse in *The Family Reunion*. It is an attempt to invest a modern setting with metaphysical significance. These metaphysical overtones are present from the very beginning. The only variation is one of emphasis and intensity. The ordered nature of the dialogue at the beginning of the play reflects the balance which is still stubbornly maintained; the stylised language towards the end is an expression of a growing loss of control. The balance has been finally upset.

In a more recent work, *Everything in the Garden* (1967), Albee returns to much the same milieu. Based on a play by the late English dramatist, Giles Cooper, this is yet another mordant attack on a society which is evidently prepared to sacrifice dignity, morality and spiritual values in the pursuit of money. Once again the playwright probes beneath the urbane surface of middle-class life to expose the greed and hypocrisy which seem to him to provide the motive force of modern society. When his protagonist is shown happily accommodating himself to a steady tax-free income derived from his wife's activities as a call girl, then clearly we are touching once again on Albee's central preoccupation with male emasculation and the subordination of the human to the material.

But Albee is no scandal-monger pandering to the prurient interests of a matinee audience. If his constant aim is to penetrate beneath the exterior of modern society to the fears and guilt which exist beneath, that is because he considers this to be the chief function of the dramatist and the main responsibility of the thinking individual. With T. S. Eliot's Agatha, he would insist that:

> we cannot rest in being
> The impatient spectators of malice and stupidity.
> We must try to penetrate the other private worlds
> Of make-believe and fear.[45]

[45] *Collected Plays*, p. 99.

CHAPTER VII

AFFIRMATION AND EXPERIMENT

In reacting against what he sees as the thinly intellectual constructs of modern European writing, Saul Bellow has frequently denounced those "comfortable people playing at crisis, alienation, apocalypse and desperation",[1] adding that "we are liable to be asked how. In what form shall life be justified. This is the essence of the moral question. We call a writer moral to the degree that his imagination indicates to us how we may answer naturally, without strained arguments, with a spontaneous mysterious proof that has no need to argue with despair."[2] This is a challenge which Albee accepts. For, although he is conscious of the accuracy of those constructs, he is also aware that they provide an incomplete picture.

Albee is concerned with modern man's attempt to relate himself to his social and metaphysical situation. He is faced on two levels with absurdity. For not only do the terms of his existence seem to justify nihilism, but his social life is founded on values which tend to undermine the very essence of his being. As he is caught up in the distractions of a materialistic society, his sense of life, meaning, and identity is gradually whittled away until he is seduced into what Heidegger has called "a forgetfulness of being".[3] Albee, indeed, is all too conscious that the interests of society and those of the individual are by no means identical, and that the aims of the group

[1] David Galloway, *The Absurd Hero in American Fiction* (London 1966), p. 132.

[2] Saul Bellow, "The Writer as Moralist", *Atlantic Monthly* (March 1963), p. 62.

[3] Herbert Kohl, *The Age of Complexity* (New York 1965), p. 133.

are frequently achieved only at the cost of individual freedom and identity. For in modern mass society, it seems, the result of this tension is no longer to produce the rebel, but rather, as the eminent sociologist Dr Hendrik Ruitenbeek has explained, to spawn men who "tend to become aimless and undirected and gradually submerge their individuality in the social character of their society ... people are led and directed and often can no longer act as individuals. Such persons", he continues, "have experienced that depersonalisation which is so strikingly a trait of modern mass culture. Appearances have become the goal; the façade counts, not what is behind it, and yet not even the façade is respected for long."[4] This, of course, is the essential theme of most of Albee's work. In fact in *Malcolm* he had described in detail precisely this disintegration of personality in the face of an absurd society. But, as we have seen, Albee finds little attraction in the contemporary cant of alienation and despair; and, if he recognises the crisis of identity through which man is passing, he does not confuse this with an enervating determinism. For to Albee the absurd does not lie in the discrepancy between the aspirations of the human spirit and the incapacity of the world to satisfy them, but in man's resolute adherence to distraction and illusion in the face of a desperate need to acknowledge reality.

Albee creates a hero who is crushed, not, like the protagonist of the naturalistic novel, by environment and heredity, nor, like the anti-hero of Beckett's plays, by the sheer weight of an indifferent universe, but by his own conscious submission. He is a self-created victim adrift in a society which has carefully constructed its own absurdity from the bricks and mortar of spiritual despair and material cupidity. If he emerges with any dignity at the end of the play, that is because Albee retains a diminishing faith in the possibility of meaningful action.

[4] *The Individual and the Crowd: A Study of Identity in America*, p. 75.

But this transformation turns on the willingness of the individual to recognise the basic terms of his own existence. For Albee is enough of an existentialist to believe that identity, human contact, and meaning are all contingent on a willingness to concede the basic facts of existence. This then is no longer a figure who runs full-tilt into society merely to prove his existence, for he is not concerned with rebellion against the essence of that existence. On the contrary, his central struggle is towards acceptance—acceptance of a world which, if smaller than the dreams and visions of false glory, is at least a real world in which other human beings offer the hope of a valid consolation. The challenge is to accept imperfection in the order of the universe and in man himself, but to place oneself in implacable opposition to everything which erodes the simple dignity of mankind. Thus Albee has fought with equal virulence the candied dreams of modern America, which worships progress while plunging into a spiritual abyss, and that despair which grants no reality to love and allows no response to life outside the merely ironical. He denies nothing of the absurdist's vision except his final collapse into solipsism or stoicism. He denies nothing of Christian morality except the Christian's need to justify that morality by reference to an abstract God.

Nevertheless, his commitment has not manifested itself primarily in political or social terms, for he is more concerned with exposing the disease than with treating the symptoms. To imagine that it is possible to cure personal and national anomie by social programmes seems to him to threaten a return to the radical simplicities of the 1920s and 1930s. Albee does not jump from one panacea to another as Strindberg or O'Neill had done. Religion, socialism, nihilism are all responses which seem to him at best irrelevant and at worst cowardly. For the essential task facing man is not the need to define his relationship to God or to a political philosophy but to himself and his fellow man. Like Ralph Ellison he believes that the key to cultural and social survival rests in the realisation of individual identity. As Karl Jaspers has pointed out, "What frees us from solitude is not the world, but the selfhood which enters into ties with others".[5]

Towards the end of his life Albert Camus declared in a lecture that he was tired of nihilism. No longer satisfied with a vision of life which left man a victim of an indifferent universe and which, incidentally, appeared to justify indiscriminate brutality, he now identified a progression which offered a viable hope. "The end of the movement of absurdity, of rebellion", he insisted, "is compassion . . . that is to say, in the last analysis, love."[6] It is this progression which Albee accepts. Starting from the premise of the absurdity of American society, he opposes its materialism with engagement and its indifference with compassion. But clearly this is no longer that innocent and bright-eyed brotherhood of man which Steinbeck had endorsed with *The Grapes of Wrath* in the 1930s, and which Arthur Miller affirmed a little unsurely with *All My Sons* in the 1940s. This is a love, as Albee stresses in *A Delicate Balance*, imperfect and tentative, sure only of the need to renew itself in the face of ultimate failure. It is a love acutely aware of the absurd, and, as the playwright Lorraine Hansberry has said, for that reason "seasoned, more cynical, tougher, harder to fool—and therefore less likely to quit".[7] If his confidence is tempered by a realistic assessment of modern man, nerveless, deluded, and largely deprived of the will to oppose the destruction of identity and compassion, he does accept the possibility of a viable response to life. He leaves man in control of his destiny

[5] Karl Jaspers, *Man in the Modern Age* (London 1951), p. 188.

[6] Albert Camus, *Carnets 1942-1951*, tr. Philip Thody (London 1966), p. 103.

[7] Lorraine Hansberry, *The Sign in Sidney Brustein's Window* (New York 1965), p. 141.

and able to construct meaning and purpose out of his relationships with his fellows. To Albee, as to Martin Buber, the gospel reads "In the beginning is relation".[8]

The American theatre has never achieved the heights of its European counterpart. Tied to the economic realities of Broadway, it has avoided experimentation almost as adroitly as it has avoided offending the susceptibilities of the theatre parties on whom its prosperity depends. In a savage little sketch called *Fam and Yam* (a dialogue between a *F*amous *Am*erican Playwright and a *Y*oung *Am*erican Playwright), Albee actually details what he sees as the source of this enervated theatre, "the theatre owners . . . ignorant, greedy, hit-happy real estate owners . . . the producers . . . opportunistic, out-for-a-buck businessmen . . . most of our playwrights are nothing better than businessmen themselves . . . out for the loot . . . our directors are slick, sleight-of-hand artists . . . the critics . . . set themselves up as sociological arbiters . . . the pin-heads . . . the theatre parties".[9] Nor was Albee by any means alone in this view, which was shared, not only by Eric Bentley (*The Playwright as Thinker*) but also by Herbert Blau, for a period a co-director at Lincoln Centre. In *The Impossible Theatre* he confesses that, "Given conditions on Broadway and the flaccidity elsewhere, when serious people in the theatre seek new ideas or want to check their own, they still have to go to Europe".[10] Regrettably this has always been true, for, with the possible exception of Tennessee Williams' *A Streetcar Named Desire*, O'Neill's *Long Day's Journey into Night* and Arthur Miller's *The Crucible* America has produced little to justify any confidence in the future of its theatre. By the late 1950s things were looking particularly bleak. With Tennessee

[8] Martin Buber, *I and Thee* (Edinburgh 1966), p. 18.

[9] Edward Albee, *The Sandbox, The Death of Bessie Smith, Fam and Yam* (New York 1963), pp. 93-4.

[10] Herbert Blau, *The Impossible Theatre* (New York 1965), pp. 7-8.

Williams continuing to produce variations on a rather limited theme, and with Miller embarked on what was to be a nine-year silence, the highlight of any season was liable to be a play by the now dead O'Neill, unearthed for posthumous production. With the advent of Edward Albee, and those other young dramatists, Gelber, Richardson, and Kopit, a genuine renaissance seemed possible. But Albee alone of this group successfully transferred to Broadway, and he alone continued to extend his scope as a dramatist without retreating into privatism, as has Gelber, or into relative insignificance, as has Kopit.

Albee's gifts to the American theatre have been considerable. For not only has he brought to it a lucidity and even an acerbic wit which it had formerly lacked, but, as Gilbert Debusscher has suggested, his work constitutes a synthesis of a European and an American tradition. As I have recently pointed out elsewhere "While receiving its impetus from the experiments of the absurdists [Albee's drama] does not reflect the ironical despair which is the mark of that theatre; neither, however, does it endorse the demand for resolution and reassurance which has largely dictated the form of Broadway's naturalistic plays. Rather it is concerned with testing new structures and with re-examining the implications of realism in a way which is reminiscent of the surrealistic experiments of the nineteen-twenties." Realism, within Albee's work, "is to be interpreted as a positive dialectic rather than a style", for to him "the confrontation of reality should be seen both as the chief function of the dramatist and as the first duty of the individual".[11] Albee's value to the American theatre lies precisely in his determination to transcend the exhausted naturalism of the Broadway theatre, while establishing an existential drama committed to examin-

[11] C. W. E. Bigsby, *Confrontation and Commitment* (London 1967). p. xvi.

ing the metaphysical rather than the social or psychological problems of man.

To Robert Brustein, however, Albee is little more than
an impersonator. "Lacking a developed style or compel-
ling subject", Brustein argues, "he elected to model
himself on the more spectacular modern dramatists."[12]
In successive plays he sees him as producing nothing more
startling than somewhat weak imitations of other playwrights; Genet in *The Zoo Story*, Ionesco in *The American
Dream*, Tennessee Williams in *The Death of Bessie Smith*,
Strindberg, O'Neill, Pirandello and Genet in *Who's
Afraid of Virginia Woolf?* and in *Tiny Alice*, Dürrenmatt,
Genet, Strindberg, Eliot, Williams, Greene and Enid
Bagnold. (Albee himself has helpfully added Sophocles
and Noel Coward.) In essence, though, this is to say no
more than that Albee is concerned with themes which
have been the traditional subject of Western literature;
the tension between illusion and reality, the debate
between free-will and determinism and the gulf between
the individual's aspirations and his existential situation.
Albee has certainly been influenced by many if not all of
those on Brustein's list, but this hardly makes him any
more of an impersonator than, say, Genet or O'Neill, for
whom similar lists could be adduced. Rather he is that
rarity in the American theatre, a playwright who is
conscious of an experimental European drama and who
remains personally dedicated to examining the potential
of his own craft. He has taken entirely seriously Ibsen's
remark that "every new creative work has the task of
shifting the boundary stakes",[13] and, at the risk of
alienating the public and critics alike, has remained
committed to radical experimentation. If this has on
occasions proved somewhat disastrous, as with *Malcolm*,
and, perhaps, *Tiny Alice*, that is a small price to pay for

[12] Robert Brustein, *Seasons of Discontent* (London 1966), pp. 155-6.
[13] Eric Bentley, *The Playwright as Thinker* (New York 1955),
p. xvi.

renewed vigour in a theatre which a decade ago was fading into insignificance.

As his most recent work, *Box-Mao-Box* (1968), points out, in a time in which our very existence is threatened we can scarcely ignore the need to create something positive and vital, in terms of personal relationships and in terms of art. Yet art itself appears to be in a state of decline. It is "all craft now . . . and going further". In the face of such a collapse of purpose and will, the work of a writer such as Albee becomes doubly significant. He recognises the need both for a reconstruction of genuine humanity and a reconstitution of valid drama. For when "art begins to hurt . . . it's time to look around. When the beauty of art reminds us of loss rather than the attainable, when it tells us what we cannot have . . . when art hurts . . . then corruption is complete."[14]

[14] Jack Kroll, "Inside the Cube", *Newsweek*, 18 Mar. 1968, p. 109.

BIBLIOGRAPHY

Note

Where two or more editions are listed, references in footnotes are to those marked * in this Bibliography. C.L.M. = The Choate Literary Magazine.

I. EDWARD ALBEE

1. Plays

Schism. In *C.L.M.*, XXXII (1946), pp. 87-110.
The American Dream and The Zoo Story. *New York (Signet) 1963; *The Zoo Story and Other Plays*, London (Cape) 1962.
The Sandbox, The Death of Bessie Smith (with *Fam and Yam*). New York (Signet) 1963.
Who's Afraid of Virginia Woolf? New York (Atheneum) 1962; *Harmondsworth (Penguin) 1965.
The Ballad of the Sad Café. New York (Atheneum) 1963; *London (Cape) 1965.
Tiny Alice. New York (Atheneum) 1965.
Malcolm. New York (Atheneum) 1966.
A Delicate Balance. New York (Atheneum) 1966.

2. Short Stories

"L'Après-midi d'un faune." In *C.L.M.*, XXXI (1954), pp. 43-4.
"Empty Tea." In *C.L.M.*, XXI (1945), pp. 53-9.
"A Place on the Water." In *C.L.M.*, XXXII (1945), pp. 15-18.
"Sort of a Test." In *C.L.M.*, XXXII (Nov. 1945), pp. 45-7.
"Well, It's Like This." In *C.L.M.*, XXXII (1945), pp. 31-4.
"Lady With an Umbrella." In *C.L.M.*, XXXII (1946), pp. 5-10.

3. Poetry

"Old Laughter." In *C.L.M.*, XXXI (1944), pp. 37-8.
"To a Gold Chain Philosopher at Luncheon." In *C.L.M.*, XXXI (1945), p. 34.
"To Whom it may Concern." In *C.L.M.*, XXXI (1945), p. 61.
"Associations." In *C.L.M.*, XXXI (1945), pp. 15-16.
"Frustration," and "Sonnet". In *C.L.M.*, XXXI (1945), p. 60.
"Question." In *C.L.M.*, XXXI (1945), p. 81.

"Eighteen." In *Kaleidograph*, XVII (1945), p. 15.
"Monologue", "The Atheist", and "Sonnet". In *C.L.M.*, XXXII (1945), p. 10.
"Reunion." In *C.L.M.*, XXXII (1945), pp. 71-2.
"Interlude." In *C.L.M.*, XXXII (1946), p. 29.
"To a Maniac." In *C.L.M.*, XXXII (1946), p. 71.
"Nihilist." In *C.L.M.*, XXXII (1946), p. 22.

4. Miscellaneous

"Richard Strauss." In *C.L.M.*, XXXI (1945), pp. 87-93.
"Chaucer: The Legend of Phyllis." In *C.L.M.*, XXXII (1945), pp. 59-63.
"A Novel Beginning." In *Esquire*, LX (1963), pp. 59-60.
"Which Theatre is the Absurd One?" In John Gassner, *Directions in Modern Theatre and Drama*, New York 1965, pp. 329-36.
"Creativity and Commitment." In *Saturday Review*, 4 Jan. 1966.

5. Interviews

DIEHL, DIGBY: "Edward Albee Interviewed." In *Transatlantic Review*, 13 (Summer 1963), pp. 57-72.
STEWART, R. S: "John Gielgud and Edward Albee Talk about the Theatre." In *Atlantic*, 215.4 (Apr. 1965), pp. 61-8.
FLANAGAN, WILLIAM: "The Art of the Theatre IV. Edward Albee." In *The Paris Review*, 39 (Fall 1966), pp. 92-121.

II. OTHERS

ANON: "Albee." In *The New Yorker*, 25 Mar. 1961, p. 31.
ANON: "Albee: Odd Man in on Broadway." In *Newsweek*, 4 Feb. 1963, pp. 49-52.
ANON: "Towards a Theatre of Quality." In *T.L.S.*, 27 Feb. 1964, p. 166.
BAXANDALL, LEE: "The Theatre of Edward Albee." In *Tulane Drama Review*, IX (1965), pp. 19-40.
BRUSTEIN, ROBERT: "The Playwright as Impersonator." In *New Republic*, 16 Nov. 1963, pp. 28-9.
——: "Albee's Allegory of Innocence." In *New Republic*, 29 Jan. 1966, pp. 36-7.
CHESTER, ALFRED: "Edward Albee: Red Herrings and White Whales." In *Commentary*, 35 (1963), pp. 296-301.
CLURMAN, HAROLD: "Theatre." In *The Nation*, 27 Oct. 1962, pp. 273-4.
CORRIGAN, ROBERT: "*Malcolm* Didn't Mean Very Much." In *Vogue*, 15 Feb. 1966, p. 56.

FRANZBLAU, ABRAHAM: "A Psychiatrist Looks at *Tiny Alice*." I
 Saturday Review, 30 Jan. 1965, p. 39.

GILMAN, RICHARD: "Skin Deep." In *Newsweek*, 30 Oct. 1966
 p. 98.

GOODMAN, HENRY: "The New Dramatists: 4, Edward Albee." I
 Drama Survey, II (1962), pp. 72-9.

HAMILTON, KENNETH: "Mr. Albee's Dream." In *Queen'*
 Quarterly, LXX (1963), pp. 393-9.

HARRIS, WENDELL: "Morality, Absurdity and Albee." I
 Southwest Review, 49 (1964), pp. 249-56.

HEWES, HENRY: "The *Tiny Alice* Caper." In *Saturday Review*, 30 Jan.
 1965, pp. 38-9, 65.

KROLL, JACK: "Inside the Cube." In *Newsweek*, 18 Mar. 196
 pp. 109-10.

LEWIS, ALLEN: " The Fun and Games of Edward Albee." I
 Educational Theatre Journal, XVI (1964), pp. 29-39; reprinted
 Plays and Playwrights of the Contemporary Theatre, New York, 196

LYONS, CHARLES: "Two Projections of the Isolation of the Huma
 Soul: Brecht's *In Dickicht der Staedte* and Albee's *The Zoo Story*
 In *Drama Survey*, IV, pp. 121-38.

MACDONALD, DANIEL: "Truth and Illusion in *Who's Afraid*
 Virginia Woolf?" In *Renascence*, XVII (1964) pp. 63-9.

MARKUS, THOMAS B.: "*Tiny Alice* and Tragic Catharsis." In
 Educational Theatre Journal, XVII (1965), pp. 225-33.

MILLER, JORDAN Y.: "Myth and the American Dream: O'Ne
 to Albee." In *Modern Drama*, VII (1964), pp. 190-8.

SAMUELS, CHARLES THOMAS: "The Theatre of Edward Albee
 In *Massachusetts Review*, VI (1964-5), pp. 187-201.

SCHNEIDER, ALAN: "Reality is Not Enough." In *Tulane Dra*
 Review, IX (1965) pp. 118-52.

TROTTA, GERI: "On Stage: Edward Albee." In *Horizon*, IV (196
 p. 79.

WOLFE, PETER: "The Social Theatre of Edward Albee." In
 Prairie Schooner, XXXIX (1965), pp. 248-52.